# The
# curious world of
# CHRISTMAS

# The
# curious world of
# CHRISTMAS

## Celebrating All That Is Weird,
## Wonderful, and Festive

## Niall Edworthy

A PERIGEE BOOK

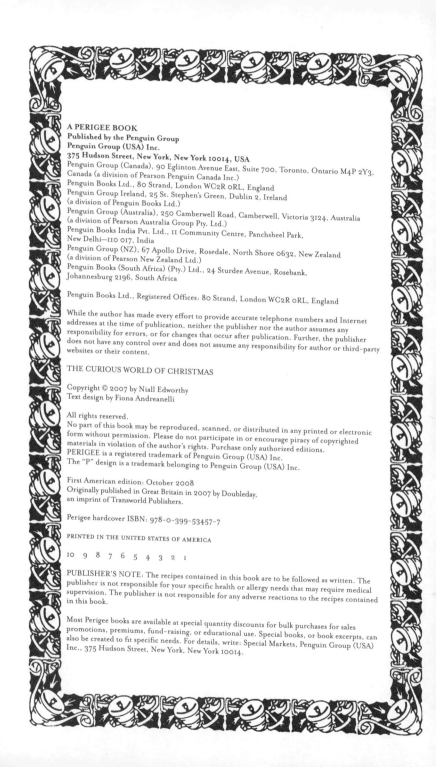

A PERIGEE BOOK
Published by the Penguin Group
Penguin Group (USA) Inc.
375 Hudson Street, New York, New York 10014, USA
Penguin Group (Canada), 90 Eglinton Avenue East, Suite 700, Toronto, Ontario M4P 2Y3,
Canada (a division of Pearson Penguin Canada Inc.)
Penguin Books Ltd., 80 Strand, London WC2R 0RL, England
Penguin Group Ireland, 25 St. Stephen's Green, Dublin 2, Ireland
(a division of Penguin Books Ltd.)
Penguin Group (Australia), 250 Camberwell Road, Camberwell, Victoria 3124, Australia
(a division of Pearson Australia Group Pty. Ltd.)
Penguin Books India Pvt. Ltd., 11 Community Centre, Panchsheel Park,
New Delhi—110 017, India
Penguin Group (NZ), 67 Apollo Drive, Rosedale, North Shore 0632, New Zealand
(a division of Pearson New Zealand Ltd.)
Penguin Books (South Africa) (Pty.) Ltd., 24 Sturdee Avenue, Rosebank,
Johannesburg 2196, South Africa

Penguin Books Ltd., Registered Offices: 80 Strand, London WC2R 0RL, England

While the author has made every effort to provide accurate telephone numbers and Internet
addresses at the time of publication, neither the publisher nor the author assumes any
responsibility for errors, or for changes that occur after publication. Further, the publisher
does not have any control over and does not assume any responsibility for author or third-party
websites or their content.

THE CURIOUS WORLD OF CHRISTMAS

First American edition: October 2008
Originally published in Great Britain in 2007 by Doubleday,
an imprint of Transworld Publishers.

Perigee hardcover ISBN: 978-0-399-53457-7

PRINTED IN THE UNITED STATES OF AMERICA

10  9  8  7  6  5  4  3  2  1

PUBLISHER'S NOTE: The recipes contained in this book are to be followed as written. The
publisher is not responsible for your specific health or allergy needs that may require medical
supervision. The publisher is not responsible for any adverse reactions to the recipes contained
in this book.

Most Perigee books are available at special quantity discounts for bulk purchases for sales
promotions, premiums, fund-raising, or educational use. Special books, or book excerpts, can
also be created to fit specific needs. For details, write: Special Markets, Penguin Group (USA)
Inc., 375 Hudson Street, New York, New York 10014.

*For Alfie and Eliza*

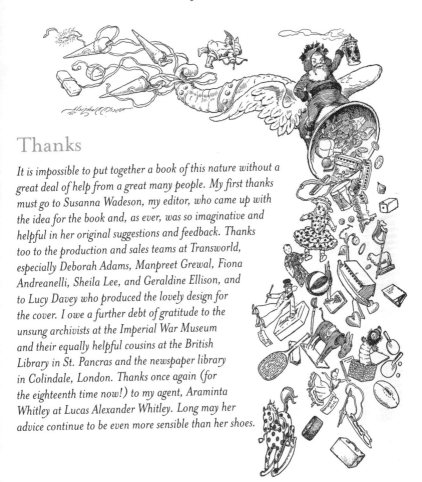

# Thanks

It is impossible to put together a book of this nature without a great deal of help from a great many people. My first thanks must go to Susanna Wadeson, my editor, who came up with the idea for the book and, as ever, was so imaginative and helpful in her original suggestions and feedback. Thanks too to the production and sales teams at Transworld, especially Deborah Adams, Manpreet Grewal, Fiona Andreanelli, Sheila Lee, and Geraldine Ellison, and to Lucy Davey who produced the lovely design for the cover. I owe a further debt of gratitude to the unsung archivists at the Imperial War Museum and their equally helpful cousins at the British Library in St. Pancras and the newspaper library in Colindale, London. Thanks once again (for the eighteenth time now!) to my agent, Araminta Whitley at Lucas Alexander Whitley. Long may her advice continue to be even more sensible than her shoes.

# Contents

# Love It or Loathe It

Introduction

IT IS A GREAT PARADOX OF CHRISTMAS THAT IT SHOULD PROMISE US all a period of tremendous harmony, peace, and fun, and yet, to a minority in our midst, it somehow manages to deliver nothing but anxiety and ill-feeling. For the Christmas grumblers, the annual winter holiday is not a generous gift in life's stocking, it's a lump of coal; a holiday period so intolerable that a return to the drudgery and routine of the workplace in the dark days of January never comes soon enough. These curmudgeons are the direct descendants of the dramatist George Bernard Shaw, whose feverish denunciations of the festive season always came speckled with a shower of froth: *"I am sorry to have to introduce the subject of Christmas,"* the Irishman spat. *"It is an indecent subject; a cruel, gluttonous subject; a wicked, cadging, lying, filthy, blasphemous, and demoralizing subject."*

With his long white beard and dancing eyes he may well have looked like Santa's skinny younger brother, but no one in history has despised Christmas quite as intensely as Shaw. Not even the seventeenth-century Puritans, who went so far as to ban its celebration for fifteen years. Nor the billions of non-Christians, who choose to ignore it, tolerate it, or look upon it from a distance with a mildly bemused indifference. (The Japanese, bless them, even join in the celebrations.)

As a socialist, Shaw was riled by the materialism and consumerism of the holiday period and what he saw as an all-too-brief flash of middle-class charity toward the poor and less fortunate; as an atheist turned mystic, he must have been repelled by the overtly Christian dimension of the holiday; as a radical rationalist, he will no doubt have been appalled by its superstitious pagan elements and the absurdity of Father Christmas and his airborne reindeer. As a serious dramatist and man of letters, he was horrified by the immense silliness of the Christmas pantomime—and all the other quaint, unintellectual, sentimental, and indulgent aspects that the season brings us by the sleigh-load. As a devout vegetarian and teetotaler, perhaps it was his physical disgust at the thought of all that roasted animal flesh and booze that excited his bile.

No one has articulated their scorn for Christmas quite as powerfully or wittily as Shaw, but there has always been a very vocal minority who share at least some of his views on the subject and no doubt there always will be. In a strange way, the Christmas moaners have become as much a feature of the season as a turkey dinner or a well-decorated tree. Somehow it wouldn't be quite the same without them.

There is, of course, another type of Christmas extremist, an altogether happier chap for whom the annual winter holiday is a perfectly smashing, absolutely fantastic occasion. He is the Christmas fanatic who will beat you over the head with turkey drumsticks until he pops out of his Santa suit if you so much as whisper a word of weariness about the world's largest religious festival. He is simply nutty for Noël. (I say "he"

advisedly because these "crazy"
Christmas cavorters are rarely
female.) You can spot a Noël
Nutter from 100 paces. He will
be the one at the Christmas party
wearing some combination of
the following: (a) a sweater or
tie with a pattern of reindeers
mating; (b) comedy glasses which
squirt snow and then wipe the
lenses with built-in wipers; and
(c) a revolving bow tie.

In all likelihood, the Noël Nutter's front lawn—and probably
his roof—will be crammed with every imaginable item of Christmas
kitsch: an eight-foot-high light-up inflatable snowman, a Santa
sleigh with a full set of reindeer and faux presents, several thousand
outdoor lights, and a road sign reading "Santa Stop Here!" *Christmas
Moron*, I think, is the proper scientific term for this species, and I'm
not sure I'd invite him around for a Christmas drink any sooner
than I would the whiners in the Shaw camp. To some extent, the
Christmas Moron is the very reason why the Shavian moaners come
over all gloomy and break out in a rash each December. Remove the
Moron—and all who encourage and sell to him—and you remove a
great deal of the reason to dislike Christmas.

Somewhere in between these two groups of extremists who have
unwittingly joined forces and done their best to despoil the image of
our ancient winter festival, you
will find the rest of us: a vast
global population of people
living in predominantly
Christian cultures for whom
Christmas remains, by and
large, and if celebrated properly, a truly
joyful period of the year.

On a superficial level, Christmas is a
time when the ordinary rules of daily life
are suspended for a week or two, when
the tools of work are laid down and the
workplace vacated, when scattered families
and old friends gravitate to each other's

homes to exchange gifts and greetings, when miserable diets and boring exercise programs are abandoned and we can eat and drink ourselves daft, when strangers treat each other with greater kindness and civility, when fireplaces, candles, and decorations bring some warmth and cheer against the cold and bleak landscape outside, when a sense of brotherhood and kindness toward the less fortunate is roused, when television and theater try even harder to entertain us, when fair-weather and lapsed Christians can enjoy going to church without feeling a little uncertain as to whether or not they should be there…. For the truly devout among us, the Christmas period is of course a wonderful and highly significant time in the calendar, even without any of the above. Falling where it does, the Christmas holiday period also has the virtue of drawing a line under one year and stirring up promise and hope for another, wiping clean the slate of our experience, and allowing us to start all over again and take another stab at getting our lives right. Christmas also acts as a milestone, or a marker, in our family lives, tracking our development and relationships over the years.

These are all great reasons to look forward to Christmas and to cherish every day of it when it comes, and when the often stressful business of preparing, organizing, and staging it allows. But it seems there is something far deeper at work in this anticipation and enjoyment, something more than plain physical indulgence and holiday-time recreation. What is it about the sound of a distant carol floating on the air, the smell of a freshly carved turkey or a pot of spiced cider, or the sight of a snowbound landscape or a tastefully decorated pine tree that excites, for so many of us, such feelings of warmth, reassurance, and expectation? The answer, I think, is found in the past: the past of our own lives *and* in the wider, deeper past of our civilization, our history, our roots.

On the face of it, December 25 is a date in a religious calendar when Christians celebrate the birth of Christ, a central day of religious observation that has expanded into a longer, more secularized holiday period. The truth, however, is far more complicated and interesting. Most of us are dimly aware that there are elements of pagan ritual blended into the Christian and commercialized secular customs of the holiday. It is well known, for instance, that the practice of hanging up mistletoe in our homes has some connection with the Druids. What I hadn't understood before setting out to research this collection was quite *how many* of our Christmas traditions are pagan in origin, stretching back thousands of years, deep into the past of European civilization. These ancient customs, many of them linked to winter solstice festivals, were

absorbed into the Christian experience. Over the centuries they have been modified, molded, and repackaged to the point where we now think of them as being mainly Christian in origin, with just a hint of paganism about them.

In truth, it's the other way around. There is no criticism of the Church, or disappointment, in this observation. On the contrary, I find it exciting that whenever we bring a Christmas tree or some holly branches into our homes, when we exchange gifts with one another, when we light our candles and fires, when we throw a Christmas party or lay on a feast, we are performing a modern-day version of our distant ancestors' winter celebrations. I may not wear an animal-skin loincloth or live in a wattle-and-daub hut or hunt and gather my own food—well, not since my university days at any rate—but the way I celebrate Christmas links me, through dozens of centuries, with my primeval forebears. Over the centuries, various cultures and civilizations have contributed to the constantly changing nature of Christmas: Romans, Persians, Celts, Norsemen, medieval kings and noblemen, Puritans and Parliamentarians, enterprising Victorians, German princes, American settlers, to name but some. I cannot think of any other event that manages to connect us to our earliest

roots as directly as all the rituals of Christmas.

Above all else, though, Christmas is about children and it is this association with innocence, the link with our own childhood, that is the most evocative and emotive aspect of the season. Our prime concern as adults is that the children, especially the younger ones, have a memorable and happy time. It's difficult not to share their sense of mounting excitement as the year advances and first the Christmas period and then the day itself approaches. (By the same token, it's easy to understand why people without children rarely show great enthusiasm for Christmas; I wonder whether it's significant that Bernard Shaw never produced a family.) By entering into the spirit of Christmas, we allow ourselves to indulge briefly in a world of innocence and in a childlike sense of wonder. That purity of feeling was stolen from us when we became world-weary grown-ups, but at Christmas we can suspend our skepticism and cynicism, forget the harsher world of adult experience for a while, surrender ourselves to sentimentality, and join in the awe and the wonder and the excitement. In short, we become children again. There's nothing cool or clever about liking Christmas, and that, I suspect, is what I like about it. I'm with Charles Dickens, not Bernard Shaw, on this one: *"Christmas time! That man must be a misanthrope indeed in whose breast something like a jovial feeling is not roused—in whose mind some pleasant associations are not awakened—by the recurrence of Christmas."*

# Farting Dwarves and Peacock Pie

## How Our Ancestors Celebrated Christmas

THE DATE OF CHRIST'S BIRTH HAS BEEN a matter of dispute for centuries, but most scholars agree that December 25 is a suspiciously convenient point in the calendar. The date just happens to be the day of the winter solstice in the old Julian calendar, when pagans across Europe and the Middle East celebrated the birth of the new sun with a series of ceremonies, feasts, and wild parties. It also marked the end of  the Roman feast of Saturnalia, a weeklong celebration in honor of Saturn, the god of agriculture and plenty. Natalis Solis Invicti ("the day of the birth of the unconquered sun") was an especially popular holiday throughout the Roman Empire. The early Church struggled to eradicate ancient pagan traditions such as the solstice celebrations and, though we cannot be certain, it seems likely that the authorities thought it sensible to absorb and then shape the various winter festivals into a Christian form, rather than alienate people by banishing them altogether.

❄ ❄ ❄ ❄

THE ROMAN HOLIDAY OF **SATURNALIA** HAD DEVELOPED INTO A WILD festival starting on December 17 and ending with the winter solstice celebrations, during which time only cooks and bakers were allowed to work. Even slaves were freed from their duties to join in the revelry, which included street processions, fire and torch ceremonies, lavish feasts, dressing up in animal skins and other costumes, and a great deal of drinking. There followed a few days' break to recuperate before the Romans launched themselves into the **Kalends** celebrations, the equivalent of our New Year, which rivaled Saturnalia for revelry and drunkenness. During the end-of-year holiday the Romans also exchanged gifts and decorated their homes with evergreens, just as we do at Christmas today.

Handily, many of the Roman traditions of Saturnalia lent themselves to Christian interpretation. The holly with which people bedecked their homes came to represent Christ's crown of thorns, and the giving of presents was a symbol of Jesus Christ as God's gift to man. Even the pagan tradition of scattering corn and straw throughout the home was easily Christianized because it reminded worshippers of Christ's lowly surroundings in the Bethlehem stable.

❄ ❄ ❄ ❄

NOWHERE IN THE GOSPELS OR THE WRITINGS of the early Christians is there any mention of Christ's birthday. It was several centuries after his lifetime that the date became a matter of conjecture and argument. This was partly because **early Christians had no interest in birthdays**. The Epiphany (today, January 6) was of greater importance: in the Eastern Churches, this was the day for celebrating Christ's baptism; in the West it was to commemorate the manifestation of Christ's glory and his revelation to the Magi. Some early Christians even took exception to the recognition of birthdays because it distracted from their more significant "deathdays," when saints were martyred and Christ had given his life for mankind. Exactly when the Church decided upon December 25 as the birth date of Jesus is unclear, but it almost certainly came to be accepted as that during the fourth century, possibly during the reign of Constantine, the first Christian Roman emperor.

*The ancient peoples of the Angli began the year on the 25th of December when we now celebrate the birthday of the Lord; and the very night which is now so holy to us, they called in their tongue "modranecht," that is, the mother's night, by reason we suspect of the ceremonies which in that night-long vigil they performed.*

ST. BEDE (c. 673–735)
*De Temporum Ratione*

❄ ❄ ❄ ❄

*The outgoing of the Romans and the incoming of the Angles, the Saxons and the Jutes, disastrously affected the festival of Christmas, for the invaders were heathens, and Christianity was swept westward before them. They lived in a part of the Continent which had not been reached by Christianity nor classic culture and they worshipped the false gods of Woden and Thunder and were addicted to various heathenish practices, some of which are mingled with the festivities of Christmastide.... The Anglo-Saxon excesses are referred to by some of the old chroniclers, intemperance being a very prevalent vice at the Christmas festival. Ale and mead were their favourite drinks; wines were used as occasional luxuries.*

W. F. DAWSON
*Christmas: Its Origins and Associations,* 1902

❄ ❄ ❄ ❄

IN THE MIDDLE AGES, THE CHURCH JOINED IN THE GENERAL REVELRY at Christmas time with some very peculiar and irreligious traditions of its own. One such was the custom of the **Boy Bishop**. At the beginning of December, usually December 6 (St. Nicholas's Day), in cathedrals across Britain and Europe, a young choirboy was elected to be bishop until the 28th, Holy Innocents' Day. He was chosen either by the bishop or by his fellow choristers, depending on the cathedral, and for three weeks the young boy, dressed in cope and mitre and carrying a crook, traveled the diocese with his high-pitched soprano chums, carrying out a number of grown-up duties. The election of the boy drew huge crowds to the cathedral and there was much hilarity as the senior clergy swapped places with the choristers. After the service, there followed a lavish feast at which the choristers were allowed to eat as much food and drink as much wine as they wished. This was the high point of the year for medieval choristers, who led a harsh, thankless life otherwise. Their days were usually long and hard, they were often fed poorly, and they were frequently beaten by their masters. During his travels, the Boy Bishop visited monasteries and larger churches, preaching sermons written for him by a senior clergyman. The tradition of the Boy Bishop was disliked by many within the Church, but others justified it on the grounds that it demonstrated vividly how the lowly and meek were able to acquire authority and respect, just as Jesus had done in his life. The Boy Bishop tradition was ended in Britain during the reign of Queen Elizabeth I, but continued for almost another 200 years elsewhere in Europe.

❊　❊　❊　❊

THE MEAT OF THE PEACOCK IS TOUGH, DRY, AND UNAPPETIZING but that didn't seem to bother the royals and nobles of the Middle Ages. To them, the Indian forest bird was a spectacular specialty, and it was served up in the dining halls of castles and baronial homes amid great pomp and ceremony. Often the bird was made into a large pie with the head sticking out through the crust at one end and its huge feathery tail sticking out of the other. Cooks sometimes discarded the meat of the peacock altogether and filled the pies with tastier birds such as goose and chicken.

❊　❊　❊　❊

CHRISTMAS DAY 1066: "THE BASTARD" BECAME "THE CONQUEROR" when William I was crowned King of England at Westminster Abbey. When the Norman contingent at the ceremony was asked by Ealdred, the Archbishop of York, if they welcomed William as king, the shouts of approval were so loud that the guards outside suspected treachery of some kind and immediately set about torching nearby buildings. Historian Orderic Vitalis records that the fire spread so fast that most of the congregation fled: *"Only the bishops and a few clergy and monks remained, terrified in the sanctuary, and with difficulty completed the*

*consecration of the king who was trembling from head to foot."* William's funeral in Caen Abbey 21 years later was no less dramatic. William's corpse, too fat for his coffin, burst midway through the service, filling the abbey with "an unbearable stench," according to Vitalis.

CAROL SINGERS were generally shunned by medieval clergy and barred from most churches on the grounds that the practice was more pagan than Christian. The carolers, who danced in a circle as they sang, were forced to pursue their revelry out in the streets, moving from house to house.

❄ ❄ ❄ ❄

DECEMBER 28 IS **"HOLY Innocents' Day"** or "Childermass Day," when the Church commemorates the children allegedly killed on the order of King Herod. It has been regarded as a day of ill omen from the Middle Ages onwards. Edward IV of England postponed his coronation to another day and Louis XI of France refused to conduct business on it, while superstitious people claim that no one should be married or start building a house on the dreaded day. Some records suggest that young English boys were beaten on Holy Innocents' Day to remind them of Herod's savagery.

❄ ❄ ❄ ❄

"WAITS" (TOWN PIPERS) were a common sight and sound from medieval times until the early nineteenth century, when an Act of Parliament forced them to lay down their noisy wind instruments. Every city and town of significance had a **band of waits** and their duties included heralding the arrival of royal guests at the town gates, or leading the mayor's parades. Their habit of wandering the streets in the dead of night and striking up a windy tune under people's windows wasn't universally appreciated, and there were few protests when the Municipal Corporations Act of 1835 forced their abolition. Like a bad smell, however, the waits lingered in the air a while longer, turning up at Christmas time to sing and play carols for money until the early twentieth century.

❄ ❄ ❄ ❄

*The only music I have heard this week is waits; to sit up working until two or three in the morning, and then—just as I am losing myself in my first sleep—to hear "Venite Adoremus" welling forth from a cornet English pitch, a saxhorn Society of Arts pitch (or thereabouts), and a trombone French pitch, is the sort of thing that breaks my peace and destroys my goodwill towards men!*

Diaries of GEORGE BERNARD SHAW (1856-1950), Irish dramatist and essayist

THE EXPRESSION "HUMBLE PIE" originates from a medieval Christmas practice whereby the rich gave the innards of their deer to the poor as a treat. The offal was known as the "umbles," and the grateful peasants used it to make a pie. Christmas Day was not all unfettered joy in the hovels of the poor, as it happened to be one of the calendar's four "quarter days" when tenants were obliged to pay his lordship his rent and taxes.

❄ ❄ ❄ ❄

DURING THE MIDDLE AGES, THE tables of the rich would have been filled with a sumptuous display of foods throughout the twelve days of Christmas. **Goose** was a common dish and the bird was often given a shiny, golden appearance by basting it

in a mixture of butter and the highly coveted and expensive spice saffron. **Pork or wild boar** often formed the pièce de résistance of the Christmas feast, and the roasts were carried into the dining halls amid great fanfare with lemons stuffed into the beasts' mouths.

❄ ❄ ❄ ❄

THE MURDER IN 1170 OF THE Archbishop of Canterbury, **Thomas à Becket**, as he prayed in his cathedral was considered all the more horrendous for its having occurred during the Christmas period. Taking King Henry II's plea—"Will no one rid me of this turbulent priest?"—to its logical conclusion, four knights of his court rode straight to Canterbury on December 29 and murdered Becket in the cathedral's north transept.

❄ ❄ ❄ ❄

IF YOUR CHILDREN MOAN AS YOU drag them away from their toys and off to church on Christmas Day, remind them of the experiences suffered by their youthful ancestors in the Middle Ages. "Christ's Mass," the celebration of the Nativity established in the seventh century, consisted of **three services**: one at midnight (the Angel's Mass), one at dawn (the Shepherd's Mass), and the third at some point during the day (the Mass of the Divine Word).

FROM WILLIAM THE CONQUEROR THROUGH TO THE EARLY SEVENTEENTH century, the feast of the Epiphany, on January 6, was celebrated far more lavishly than Christmas Day owing to its associations with the notion of kingship. It is the day that the Church celebrated the showing of Christ "the King" to the Three Kings, Caspar, Melchior, and Balthazar. For centuries and until modern times, in many countries it was customary to **exchange gifts on the Epiphany**, not on the Nativity.

❉ ❉ ❉ ❉

IN THE LATE TWELFTH CENTURY, HENRY II HAD A FOOL CALLED Roland le Pettour (Roland the Farter), whose antics he enjoyed so much that he used to force him out of retirement on Christmas Day to perform his *saltum, siffletum et pettum* routine (a leap, a whistle, and a fart). Two centuries on, William Langland wrote in *Piers Plowman* of minstrels **farting in harmony** with their pipes to amuse their noble patrons during the Christmas festivities.

❉ ❉ ❉ ❉

THE ROYAL CHRISTMAS FEAST OF 1214 IS A SIGNIFICANT MOMENT IN British history, for it was then that England's barons laid down their demands to King John for what became the Magna Carta.

*Janus sits by the fire with double beard,*
*And drinketh of his bugle horn the wine:*
*Before him stands the brawn of tusk-ed swine.*
*And "Nowel" cryeth every lusty man.*

CHAUCER's only reference to Christmas, in "The Franklin's Tale"
*Canterbury Tales*

❄ ❄ ❄ ❄

WHEN RICHARD II ENTERTAINED KING LEON OF ARMENIA AT THE ROYAL
Palace, Eltham, over Christmas 1386, he laid on a **feast** of great
extravagance, feeding 10,000 guests over twelve days with 28 oxen,
300 sheep, and thousands of game birds and fowl.

❄ ❄ ❄ ❄

DURING HIS SIEGE OF ROUEN IN 1418, HENRY V SUSPENDED OPERATIONS
on Christmas Day and delivered food for the hungry inhabitants.

❄ ❄ ❄ ❄

UNTIL THE NINETEENTH CENTURY PEOPLE USED TO KEEP UP THEIR
**holly and ivy**, and other evergreen decorations, until Candlemas on
February 2, which officially marks the end of the Christmas period
according to the Christian calendar. Candlemas commemorates the
ritual purification of Mary, 40 days after Christ's birth, and evolved
from an ancient Jewish belief that women were unclean after the birth
of a child. Women weren't allowed to worship in the temple for 40
days after giving birth to a boy and for 60 days if it was a girl, after
which they had to
be cleansed.
It is known as
Candlemas because
it was on this day that all the church's
candles for the year were blessed, and many
homes placed candles on their windowsills.
Like many Christmas traditions, Candlemas
was a bastardized Christian version of a pagan
tradition. For centuries, millennia even, pagans had
celebrated the festival of light at this time of year as
it marked the halfway point of winter, between
the winter solstice and the spring equinox.

FROM THE MIDDLE AGES TO THE Tudor period, the English monarch traditionally invited dozens of the nobility to join the royal court in lavish and lengthy celebrations over the Christmas period. Great offense was given by those who declined the invitation, and the only acceptable excuses were war, childbirth, and life-threatening illness. Queen Elizabeth I was especially insistent that her male courtiers left their wives at home and joined her for the full twelve days of festivities. A royal banquet could feature as many as twenty courses, and kitchens were obliged to cook far more than the guests could eat so that a generous surplus might be distributed to the poor when their lordships could eat or drink no more, and had moved on to tossing the court dwarves and throwing scraps to the minstrels. Often, the local townsfolk were allowed into the dining hall to put on a sort of **variety performance** for the King or Queen, featuring jugglers, magicians, mimes, musicians, and bards.

❄ ❄ ❄ ❄

THE FEAST OF FOOLS, LIKE THE TRADITION OF THE BOY BISHOP, was a bizarre medieval Christmas practice that can have done little to promote the dignity of the clergy. In an ecclesiastical version of an office party crossed with a pantomime, members of the lower clergy (usually peasants) dressed up as animals, women, bishops, and sometimes even the Pope, and set about mocking their higher-ranking colleagues and the Church's most sacred institutions. There was much **license and buffoonery** throughout the pageant, which usually took place on or about the Feast of the Circumcision (January 1). More often known by its Latin name, Festum Fatuorum, the festival, which was especially popular in France, was considered blasphemous by the more serious-minded within the Church. The pagan roots of the tradition, with their echoes of the raucous Roman Saturnalia, were a further cause of disquiet and the comic custom was finally forbidden, under pain of the harshest penalties, by the Council of Basle in 1435.

❋ ❋ ❋ ❋

THE CUSTOM OF SINGING CAROLS OUTSIDE people's houses dates back to medieval times when the tradition was known as **"wassailing,"** an altogether raucous activity compared to the innocent pastime we know today. The word "wassail" derives from the Old English words *wæs* and *hæl* meaning "be healthy" or "be whole." Originally, a wassail ceremony celebrated the new rising of the sun following the Winter Solstice, and encouraged a bountiful harvest of fruit in the coming year. By the 1500s, wassailing often took the form of bands of drunk peasants, staggering between the houses of richer folk, singing carols and refusing to leave until they had been rewarded for their efforts with a gift or a donation of hard cash. The wassailers' demand for "figgy pudding" in the traditional carol "We Wish You a Merry Christmas" is followed up by the menacing "We won't go until we get some!"

❋ ❋ ❋ ❋

THE TRADITIONAL "WASSAIL" DRINK ENJOYED BY OUR FOREBEARS comprised a mixture of **mulled ale, spices, and the pulp of roasted apples**—and, it seems, anything else that was lying around, including curdled cream and eggs. The frothiness of the concoction explains its alternative name of "lamb's wool." There are still odd pockets of die-hard wassailers to be found, defiantly singing and dancing beneath apple trees, performing curious quasi-pagan rituals, and drinking to the health of apple trees in the hope that they may produce a better cider crop. The custom often takes place on the old Twelfth Night, January 17.

❋ ❋ ❋ ❋

*Let every man take off his hat*
*And shout out to th' old apple tree*
*"Old apple tree we wassail thee*
*And hoping thou will bear."*

WASSAILING SONG

LIKE SO MANY MEDIEVAL CHRISTMAS TRADITIONS, WASSAILING WAS suppressed during the Puritan crackdown on fun in the seventeenth century. In 1644, Oliver Cromwell's administration carried an Act of Parliament banning any form of celebration during the Twelve Days of Christmas, on the grounds that there is no mention of Christmas in the Bible. But it was the pagan elements and "Popish" associations to which the Puritans took the most violent exception. The more extreme Puritans dubbed December 25 "Satan's working day" and the "Antichrist's Mass." They even **banned mince pies** and the traditional evergreen decorations such as holly and ivy, and "lust-inducing" mistletoe. Christmas officially became a gloomy day of work and fasting until 1660, when, to the great relief of the drinking classes, the monarchy was restored and Charles II sat on the throne. But Christmas was never quite the same again and it wasn't until the combined efforts of Prince Albert, Charles Dickens, and a handful of Americans in the nineteenth century that the festive season rediscovered its medieval sense of joy.

❄ ❄ ❄ ❄

THE PURITAN WRITER WILLIAM PRYNNE HAD THIS TO SAY ABOUT Christmas festivities in 1633: *"When our Saviour was borne into the world at first we hear of no feasting, drinking, healthing, carding, dicing, stage plays, mummeries, masques or heathenish Christmas pastimes; those puritanical angels, saints and shepherds knew no such pompous Christmas courtships which the devil and his accursed instruments have since appropriated to his most blessed Nativity."*

❄ ❄ ❄ ❄

THE DIARIST JOHN EVELYN, A PROTESTANT BUT NO PURITAN, WROTE this well-known account of his experiences when he went to observe the Nativity in a chapel off the Strand in London in 1657:

*I went to London with my wife to celebrate Christmas Day. Sermon ended, the chapel was surrounded with soldiers. As we went up to receive the Sacrament, the miscreants held their muskets against us, as if they would have shot us at the altar: but yet suffering us to finish the office of Communion, as perhaps not having instructions what to do in case they found us in that action.*

Evelyn was held for 24 hours for celebrating Christmas Day and reprimanded for his folly.

THE CALVINIST SCOTS OF THE sixteenth century were particularly severe in their denunciation of Christmas celebrations. Dourness had become a virtue north of the Tweed and never more so than when their frivolous, effete neighbors over the border were shaming themselves during December in wild, drunken revelry, lust, and gluttony. Nearly a century before the Puritans took power in England after the Civil War, **the Scots had stamped out any semblance of Christmas fun** in their own land. Not that Christmas in Scotland had been a barrel of laughs beforehand. In 1575 magistrates in Aberdeen punished a group of girls for "playing, dancing, and singing of filthy carols on Yule Day." It wasn't until 1958 that Christmas became a national holiday in Scotland.

❋　❋　❋　❋

*Perhaps no single circumstance more strongly illustrates the temper of the Precisians [Puritans] than their conduct respecting Christmas Day. Christmas had been, from time immemorial, the season of joy and domestic affection, the season when families assembled, when children came home from school, when quarrels were made up, when carols were heard in every street, when every house was decorated with evergreens, and every table was loaded with good cheer. At that season all hearts not utterly destitute of kindness were enlarged and softened. At that season the poor were admitted to partake largely of the overflowings of the wealth of the rich, whose bounty was peculiarly acceptable on account of the shortness of the days and of the severity of the weather. At that season, the interval between landlord and tenant, master and servant, was less marked than through the rest of the year. Where there is much enjoyment there will be some excess: yet, on the whole, the spirit in which the holiday was kept was not unworthy of a Christian festival.... No public act of that time seems to have irritated the common people more [than the suppression of Christmas]. On the next anniversary of the festival formidable riots broke out in many places. The constables were resisted, the magistrates insulted, the houses of noted zealots attacked, and the prescribed service of the day openly read in the churches.*

THOMAS BABINGTON MACAULAY
(1800–1859)
*The History of England from James II*

THE PILGRIMS WHO CAME TO AMERICA IN THE EARLY 1600S WERE English Puritans, and even more zealous in their beliefs than those they left behind. Christmas was not a holiday for most early settlers and from 1659 to 1681 the celebration of it was banned by the courts in Boston. When the ban was lifted, those who took to celebrating the day were regarded with contempt. In 1687, the well-known Puritan Reverend Increase Mather wrote: "*The generality of Christmas-keepers observe that festival after such a manner as is highly dishonourable to the name of Christ. How few are there comparatively that spend those holidays (as they are called) after an holy manner. But they are consumed in Compotations, in Interludes, in playing at Cards, in Revellings, in excess of Wine, in mad Mirth....*" As in England, Christmas never recovered its former glory after the Puritan purge. A century later, the House of Congress was in session on December 25, 1789, the first Christmas under America's new constitution, and it wasn't until 1870 that it was declared a federal holiday.

❄ ❄ ❄ ❄

FROM 1558, ENGLISH CATHOLICS WERE PROHIBITED BY LAW TO practice their faith for almost three centuries and it wasn't until 1829, when an Act of Parliament sealed a growing cultural tolerance, that the emancipation of the "Papists" was completed. Though some historians dispute the claim, others assert that "The Twelve Days of Christmas" was a song written as a **coded memory aid** to help young Catholics learn the basics of their faith. According to the theory:

*The partridge in the pear tree is the Son of God*

*Two turtle doves are the Old and New Testament*

*Three French hens, faith, hope, and charity*

*Four calling birds, the four Gospels*

*Five golden rings, the first five books of the Old Testament (Pentateuch) chronicling Man's fall from grace*

*Six geese a'laying, the six days of creation*

*Seven swans a'swimming, seven gifts of the Holy Spirit and the seven sacraments*

*Eight maids a'milking, the eight Beatitudes from the Sermon on the Mount ("Blessed are the meek," etc.)*

*Nine ladies dancing, nine fruits of the Holy Spirit*

*Ten lords a'leaping, Ten Commandments*

*Eleven pipers piping, eleven faithful apostles*

*Twelve drummers drumming, twelve points of doctrine in the Apostles' Creed.*

The diary of Samuel Pepys gives an insight into a middle-class Christmas in London, the year following the end of Puritan rule:

*Wednesday 25 December 1661. In the morning to church, where at the door of our pew I was fain to stay, because that the sexton had not opened the door. A good sermon of Mr. Mills. Dined at home all alone, and taking occasion from some fault in the meat to complain of my maid's sluttery, my wife and I fell out, and I up to my chamber in a discontent. After dinner my wife comes up to me and all friends again, and she and I to walk upon the leads, and there Sir W. Pen called us, and we went to his house and supped with him, but before supper Captain Cock came to us half drunk, and began to talk, but Sir W. Pen knowing his humour and that there was no end of his talking, drinks four great glasses of wine to him, one after another, healths to the king, and by that means made him drunk, and so he went away, and so we sat down to supper, and were merry, and so after supper home and to bed.*

* * * *

From the end of Puritan domination in the late seventeenth century through to the early years of Queen Victoria's reign, Christmas Day for most people occasioned **far more subdued** celebrations than New Year's Day and Twelfth Night. To many, it was a day just like any other. The *Times* newspaper in London made no mention of the day between 1790 and 1835. The Christmas period had an obvious structure at this time, beginning with the holy day of the Nativity and ending with a wilder, more indulgent festival to celebrate Twelfth Night, on the eve of the Epiphany. Right in the middle of the period, there was an entirely non-religious day of drinking and dancing to see in the New Year.

* * * *

*Christmas goes out in fine style with Twelfth Night. It is a finish worthy of the time. Christmas Day was the morning of the season; New Year's Day the middle of it, or noon; Twelfth Night is the night, brilliant with innumerable planets of Twelfth-cakes. The whole island keeps court; nay, all Christendom. All the world are kings and queens. Everybody is somebody else, and learns at once to laugh at, and to tolerate, characters different from his own, by enacting them. Cakes, characters, forfeits, lights, theatres, merry rooms, little holiday-faces, and, last not least, the painted sugar on the cakes, so bad to eat but so fine to look at, useful because it is perfectly useless except for a sight and a moral—all conspire to throw a giddy splendour over the last night of the season, and to send it to bed in pomp and colours, like a Prince.*

Leigh Hunt (1784–1859), on the Twelfth Night Cake

*We grouped ourselves round the farmhouse porch. The sky cleared and broad streams of stars ran down over the valley and away to Wales. On Slad's white slopes, seen through the black sticks of its woods, some red lamps burned in the windows.*

*Everything was quiet: everywhere there was the faint crackling silence of the winter night. We started singing, and we were all moved by the words and the sudden trueness of our voices. Pure, very clear, and breathless we sang:*

> *As Joseph was walking*
> *He heard an angel sing;*
> *This night shall be the birth-time*
> *Of Christ the Heavenly King.*
> *He neither shall be bored*
> *In House nor in hall*
> *Not in a place of paradise*
> *But in an ox's stall …*

Enthralled by his first pantomime he thought his little world was crammed tight with pleasure that night. But he was wrong. Before mother gave him his good-night kiss, she gave him his first Kia-Ora (in hot water for the night was cold). As he drained the glass to the last delicious drop, his happiness was really complete. It was the perfect end to a perfect day. Mother! It's delicious! Always ask your grocer for a bottle.

*And two thousand Christmases became real to us then; The houses, the halls, the places of paradise had all been visited; The stars were bright to guide the Kings through the snow; and across the farmyard we could hear the beasts in their stalls. We were given roast apples and hot mince pies, in our nostrils were spices like myrrh, and in our wooden box, as we headed back for the village, there were golden gifts for all.*

LAURIE LEE (1914–1997), *Cider with Rosie*

❄ ❄ ❄ ❄

*In South Cardiganshire it seems that about eighty years ago the population, rich and poor, male and female, of opposing parishes, turned out on Christmas Day and indulged in the game of football with such vigour that it became little short of a serious fight.*

SIR LAURENCE GOMME (1853–1916), folklore historian
*The Village Community*

❄ ❄ ❄ ❄

"HARK THE HERALD ANGELS SING" WAS WRITTEN IN 1739 BY CHARLES Wesley, brother of John Wesley, the founder of the Methodist Church. Many hymns written at that time were just **words without music**, and it was left to others to choose a tune suitable for the meter of the verse. Wesley imagined that his "Hark the Herald" lyrics would be sung to the same tune as his Easter hymn "Christ the Lord Is Risen Today." The tune we now sing was written by the great German composer Felix Mendelssohn in 1840 to commemorate the invention of the printing press by Johannes Gutenberg.

IN GERMAN CHURCHES OF THE EIGHTEENTH CENTURY, MIDNIGHT Christmas services were common, but they were banned in many places because the **congregation was often so drunk and bawdy** that the ceremony descended into chaos and, occasionally, into a mass brawl. Riots used to occur outside the churches before or after the service as crowds of Christmas revelers staggered back and forth from the taverns.

❄ ❄ ❄ ❄

CHRISTMAS IS SO deeply ingrained in our culture today that we can be forgiven for believing that our ancestors celebrated it, in the same way that we do, from the dawn of Christian time. It seems almost incredible that for the better part of two millennia (until the 1840s, roughly) it barely registered as a date of any great significance. Even more remarkable perhaps is the explosive manner of its nineteenth-century revival. Within no more than five to ten years, December 25 went from being a day of **quiet religious observance** for believers to a cultural phenomenon that quickly spread, through an unacknowledged alliance of missionaries and tradesmen, from Britain and America to every corner of the Christian world, and even beyond into other cultures. There were three main catalysts in its dramatic eruption into Victorian society: Charles Dickens, the royal family, and a poem by an American, Clement Clark Moore—"An Account of a Visit from St. Nicholas"—which popularized the image of the saint as an overweight, bearded old man in a red suit who traversed the globe in a sleigh pulled by reindeer and delivered gifts down the chimney.

IF ONE EVENT, MORE THAN ANY OTHER, BROUGHT ABOUT THE REVITA-lization of Christmas in Britain and the United States, while simultaneously reinventing it, it was Dickens' writing of *A Christmas Carol*. He wrote the tale of Scrooge and Tiny Tim in just two months, finishing it at the end of November 1843. When it was published on December 17, the book sold out immediately and its popularity quickly spread to the United States. The themes chimed with the feelings of the middle classes—discomfited by the poverty and destitution beyond their cozy homes—that Christmas should be about charity and goodwill to all men. Canny tradesmen were quick to exploit this sentiment among the burgeoning ranks of the better off and, within a decade, Christmas had become a highly commercialized event.

❄ ❄ ❄ ❄

*The thought of Christmas raises almost automatically the thought of Charles Dickens, and for two very good reasons. To begin with, Dickens is one of the few English writers who have actually written about Christmas.... Secondly, Dickens is remarkable, indeed almost unique, among modern writers in being able to give a convincing picture of happiness. Dickens dealt successfully with Christmas twice, in a chapter of* The Pickwick Papers *and in* A Christmas Carol. *The latter story was read to Lenin on his deathbed and according to his wife, he found its "bourgeois sentimentality" completely intolerable. Now in a sense Lenin was right: but if he had been in better health he would perhaps have*

noticed that the story has interesting sociological implications. To begin with, however thick Dickens may lay on the paint, however disgusting the "pathos" of Tiny Tim may be, the Cratchit family give the impression of enjoying themselves. They sound happy.... They are in high spirits because for once in a way they have enough to eat. The wolf is at the door, but he is wagging his tail. The steam of the Christmas pudding drifts across a background of pawnshops and sweated labour, and in a double sense the ghost of Scrooge stands beside the dinner table.... The Cratchits are able to enjoy Christmas precisely because it only comes once a year. Their happiness is convincing just because Christmas only comes once a year. Their happiness is convincing just because it is described as incomplete.

GEORGE ORWELL (1903–1950), English writer
*Can Socialists Be Happy?*

❋  ❋  ❋  ❋

*Happy, happy Christmas, that can win us back to the delusions of our childish days; that can recall to the old man the pleasures of his youth; that can transport the sailor and the traveller, thousands of miles away, back to his own fireside and his quiet home!*

CHARLES DICKENS (1812–1870)
*The Pickwick Papers*

❋  ❋  ❋  ❋

For many people, indeed, the charm of Christmas is inseparably associated with the country . . . the city is too vast, too modern, too sophisticated. It is bound up with the thought of frosty fields, of bells heard far away, of bare trees against the starlit sky, of carols sung not by trained choirs but by rustic folk with rough accent, irregular time, and tunes learnt by ear and not by book.

CLEMENT A. MILES, *Christmas Customs and Traditions* (1912)

❋  ❋  ❋  ❋

At a period of feasts, when the paupers in the Union Workhouses are embraced in the large circle of our sympathies, and cared for a little more liberally than usual, let us draw a circle around the circle, and include within it the beggars in the streets. It may be wrong, as a rule, to encourage street beggars by donations of any kind; but Christmas is an exceptional period and though, possibly, in being charitable to all we may be charitable to many worthless persons, the good Will and good Day will consecrate the deed.

*Illustrated London News*, December 1848

QUEEN VICTORIA AND HER GERMAN HUSBAND PRINCE
Albert played a major part in reviving Christmas. Following their
marriage in 1840, Victoria went to great lengths to encourage
**German Christmas customs** to make Albert feel at home in
Britain. It is thought that it was George III's German consort,
Queen Charlotte, who introduced the Christmas tree
(*Weihnachtsbaum*) to the British royal family, but it was
Albert who made it an institution. Within a year or
two, thousands of well-to-do Britons had copied the
royals and begun to decorate fir trees in their homes,
covering them in candles, toys, handmade cards, strings
of candied almonds, and small boxes containing gifts and
sweets.

❄ ❄ ❄ ❄

*'Twas Christmas broach'd the mightiest ale;*
*'Twas Christmas told the merriest tale;*
*A Christmas gambol oft could cheer*
*The poor man's heart through half the year.*

SIR WALTER SCOTT (1771–1832), Scottish novelist and poet
*Marmion*

❄ ❄ ❄ ❄

AS A CHRISTIAN WITH A STRONG SOCIAL CONSCIENCE, VICTORIA WENT
to great charitable lengths at Christmas, and the example she set was
followed by many others privileged to lead relatively comfortable
lives. In 1836, three years before her coronation, she persuaded her
mother to send provisions, blankets, and coal to a gypsy camp she
had visited, writing:

*Their being assisted makes me quite merry and*
*happy today, for yesterday night when I*
*was safe and happy at home in that cold*
*night and today when it snowed so and*
*everything looked white, I felt unhappy*
*and grieved to think that our poor gypsy*
*friends should perish and shiver from want.*

*I must now seek in the children an echo of what Ernest [his brother] and I were in the old time, of what we felt and thought; and their delight in the Christmas-trees is not less than ours used to be.*

PRINCE ALBERT (1819–1860)

AT ROUGHLY THE SAME TIME that Victoria, Albert, and Dickens—with the help of some profit-hunting tradesmen—were busily restoring and reinventing Christmas in Britain, German settlers in the United States were performing a similar role in the towns and cities of the east coast. German immigrants arrived in America in the tens of thousands in the eighteenth and nineteenth centuries, bringing with them their traditional Christmas customs, and introducing the use of **Christmas trees** to their fellow settlers. For many years, the Christmas period had been something of a drunken and riotous affair in America, occasioning serious outbreaks of disorder, but from the 1830s onwards it rapidly began to evolve into the festival we recognize today, just as it did in England.

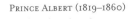

IN 1820, THE HIGHLY POPULAR AMERICAN AUTHOR WASHINGTON
Irving, under the pseudonym Geoffrey Crayon, published *The Sketch
Book*, in which there are long, **colorful, radiant descriptions** of the
joyful celebration of Christmas in England. Although Irving had
traveled extensively in England, many historians believe that, like
Dickens in *A Christmas Carol*, his descriptions were not based on his
actual experiences but were pure inventions.

*In the course of a December tour in Yorkshire, I rode for a long distance in one
of the public coaches, on the day preceding Christmas. The coach was crowded,
both inside and out, with passengers, who, by their talk, seemed principally
bound to the mansions of relations or friends to eat the Christmas dinner. It
was loaded also with hampers of game, and baskets and boxes of delicacies; and
hares hung dangling their long ears about the coachman's box—presents from
distant friends for the impending feast. I had three fine rosy-cheeked schoolboys
for my fellow passengers inside, full of the buxom health and manly spirit which
I have observed in the children of this country. They were returning home for
the holidays in high glee, and promising themselves a world of enjoyment. It
was delightful to hear the gigantic plans of pleasure of the little rogues, and the
impracticable feats they were to perform during their six weeks' emancipation
from the abhorred thraldom of book, birch, and pedagogue.*

WASHINGTON IRVING (1783–1859)
*The Sketch Book*

*Hundreds of silver toned bells of London ring loud, deep and clear from tower and spire to welcome in Christmas. The far-stretching suburbs, like glad children, take up and fling back the sound, over hill and valley, marsh and meadow, while steeple calls to steeple across the winding arms of the mast-covered river, proclaiming to the heathen voyager who has brought his treasures to our coast, and who is ignorant of our religion, the approach of some great Christian festival. Through the long night of departed centuries has that old Saxon sound pealed over our ancient City—from soon after the period when Augustin and his brother monks landed in England, with the banner borne before them, on which was emblazoned the figure of the dying Redeemer, while they moved gravely along, chanting the Holy Litany. We have often paused, with closed eyes, in some star-lighted lane in the suburbs, and listened to the sound of those sweet Christmas bells, until the imagination was borne far away to the fields of Bethlehem (flooded with heavenly light), and we fancied we again heard those angel-voices which startled the shepherds as they watched their flocks by night, while proclaiming high overhead, "Peace and goodwill towards men."*

THOMAS MILLER (1807–1874), poet and author in the Christmas edition of the
*Illustrated London News,* 1849

❄  ❄  ❄  ❄

"JINGLE BELLS" HAS BEEN A CHRISTMAS favorite for 150 years, but it was originally written for the exclusively American celebration of Thanksgiving, which takes place on the last Thursday of November. Its composer, James Pierpoint, called the song "One Horse Open Sleigh" when he wrote it in 1857, and it proved so popular at Thanksgiving that it was rolled out again a month later at Christmas and has stuck with the December celebration ever since. The song boasts the honor of being the first to be broadcast from space. In December 1965, Gemini 6 astronauts Thomas Stafford and Walter Schirra Jr. contacted Mission Control in Houston, allegedly with an important sighting. "We have an object, looks like a satellite going from north to south, probably in polar orbit," they reported. "I see a command module and eight smaller modules in front. The pilot of the command module is wearing a red suit...." The astronauts then took out a harmonica and some sleigh bells and knocked out a fairly ropey rendition of "Jingle Bells."

*Of late I have been studying with diligence the four prose poems about Christ. At Christmas I managed to get hold of a Greek Testament, and every morning, after I had cleaned my cell and polished my tins, I read a little of the Gospels, a dozen verses taken by chance anywhere. It is a delightful way of opening the day. Every one, even in a turbulent, ill-disciplined life, should do the same. Endless repetition, in and out of season, has spoiled for us the freshness, the naivete, the simple romantic charm of the Gospels. We hear them read far too often and far too badly, and all repetition is anti-spiritual. When one returns to the Greek; it is like going into a garden of lilies out of some narrow and dark house.*

OSCAR WILDE (1854–1900)
*De Profundis*

❄ ❄ ❄ ❄

**THOMASING. IN SOME RURAL DISTRICTS THE CUSTOM STILL PREVAILS OF** Thomasing—that is, of collecting small sums of money or obtaining drink from the employers of labor on the 21st of December, St. Thomas's Day.

*Brewer's Dictionary of Phrase and Fable,* 1898

❄ ❄ ❄ ❄

*There is no more dangerous or disgusting habit than that of celebrating Christmas before it comes, as I am doing in this article. It is the very essence of a festival that it breaks upon one brilliantly and abruptly, that at one moment the great day is not and the next moment the great day is.*

G. K. CHESTERTON (1874–1936)
*All Things Considered*

❄ ❄ ❄ ❄

*I must tell you what a charming day I spent at Mt. Vernon with mama and Sally. The Gen'l and Madame came home on Christmas Eve and such a racket the Servants made for they were glad of their coming! Three handsome young officers came with them. All Christmas afternoon people came to pay their respects and duty. Among these were stately dames and gay young women. The Gen'l seemed happy and Mistress Washington was from Daybreake making everything as agreeable as possible for everybody.*

ACCOUNT BY YOUNG FREDERICKSBURG
woman of Christmas spent with former
President George Washington and family

TODAY, FRANKLIN PIERCE, THE FOURTEENTH President of the United States, is chiefly remembered for being a tremendous drunk who once ran over a woman in his carriage after downing a bottle or two of strong liquor. On a happier note, perhaps, in 1856 he became the first president to place a **Christmas tree in the White House**. It wasn't until 1923, however, that the presidential tradition of lighting the National Christmas Tree from the White House was initiated—by Calvin Coolidge.

## Christmas Day Birthdays

**1717**—Pope Pius VI

**1642**—Sir Isaac Newton, *mathematician*

**1876**—Muhammad Ali Jinnah, *founder of Pakistan*

**1878**—Louis Chevrolet, *Swiss-born racing driver*

**1891**—Clarrie Grimmett, *Australian cricketer*

**1899**—Humphrey Bogart, *American actor*

**1907**—Cab Calloway, *American bandleader*

**1908**—Quentin Crisp, *English author*

**1918**—Anwar Sadat, *President of Egypt*

**1945**—Kenny Everett, *English comedian*

**1949**—Sissy Spacek, *American actress*

**1954**—Annie Lennox, *Scottish singer*

**1957**—Shane McGowan, *Irish singer*

**1971**—Dido Florian Cloud de Bounevialle Armstrong, *aka Dido, English singer*

## Christmas Day Deaths

**795**—Pope Adrian I

**1156**—Peter the Venerable, *Benedictine abbot of Cluny*

**1926**—Yoshihito, *Emperor of Japan*

**1938**—Karel Čapek, *Czech author*

**1946**—W. C. Fields, *American comedian*

**1977**—Charlie Chaplin, *English actor*

**1983**—Joan Miró, *Catalan painter*

**1989**—Nicolae Ceauşescu, *Romanian dictator*

**1995**—Dean Martin, *American singer*

**2006**—James Brown, *American singer*

*The fir tree was put into a great tub filled with sand…. The servants, and the young ladies also decked it out. On one branch they hung little nets, cut out of coloured paper; every net was filled with sweetmeats; golden apples and walnuts hung down as if they grew there, and more than a hundred little candles, red, white and blue, were fastened to the different boughs. Dolls that looked exactly like real people—the Tree had never seen such before—swung among the foliage, and high on the summit of the Tree was fixed a tinsel star. It was splendid, particularly splendid. "This evening," said all. "This evening it will shine."*

HANS CHRISTIAN ANDERSEN (1805–1875)
*The Fir Tree*

IT WAS DURING THE VICTORIAN PERIOD THAT THE **PANTOMIME**, based on the Italian traveling "harlequinades" of the previous century, began to evolve into the kitsch, slapstick productions we recognize today. The Victorians loved the pantomime, and the shows during that time became increasingly spectacular and innovative as rival theater owners vied with each other to put on the best show of the season. A great deal of mechanical ingenuity was needed to pull off a number of special effects, such as flying devices and trapdoors, while some theaters even installed giant water tanks below the stage to create water features like waterfalls, rivers, and even sea battles. Pantomime was not to everyone's taste, however….

*I am sorry to have to introduce the subject of Christmas …. It is an indecent subject; a cruel, gluttonous subject; a wicked, cadging, lying, filthy, blasphemous, and demoralizing subject. Christmas is forced on a reluctant and disgusted nation by the shopkeepers and the press: on its own merits it would wither and shrivel in the fiery breath of universal hatred; and anyone who looked back to it would be turned into a pillar of greasy sausages. Yet, though it is over now for a year, and I can go out without positively elbowing my way through the groves of carcasses, I am dragged back to it, with my soul full of loathing, by the pantomime.*

GEORGE BERNARD SHAW (1856–1950), Irish dramatist and essayist
*Our Theatres in the Nineties,* 1898

BY THE END OF THE NINETEENTH CENTURY, THE CRYSTAL PALACE, relocated to Sydenham from Hyde Park after the Great Exhibition of 1851, was staging a Christmas Variety extravaganza, which the organizers billed as "The Finest, Most Costly, and Most Varied Christmas Show in Europe!" A series of spectacular entertainments included foreign circus performers, Bedouin Arabs showing off their equestrian prowess, Japanese high-wire performers, tumbling clowns, and even a pair of **high-diving horses** from the United States. The Thoroughbreds ran up a fenced-off walkway before leaping headfirst into a pool of water.

THERE ARE TWO CHRISTMAS ISLANDS. ONE IS IN THE INDIAN OCEAN and acquired its name after it was sighted on that day in 1643 by Captain William Mynors of the British East India Company aboard the *Royal Mary*. It has a population of 1,500 and is administered by Australia. Not much happens there apart from a spot of phosphate mining. In spite of its name, only about 15 percent of the people are Christian, the rest being mainly Buddhist or Muslim. The other Christmas Island, in the Micronesia region of the Pacific Ocean, was discovered by Captain Cook on Christmas Eve, 1777. The island, which gained its independence as part of Kiribati in 1979, is the largest and oldest atoll in the world, but that didn't stop the British from carrying out nuclear tests there in the 1950s.

THE CHRISTMAS HOLIDAY PERIOD FOR **PIONEERS** LIVING IN THE WEST or the Great Plains in the mid-nineteenth century was generally a humble affair in often harsh conditions. Money was in short supply, and luxury goods, such as cakes, candies, and gifts, were only to be found back in the thriving towns and cities of the Eastern seaboard.

Ferocious blizzards blasted across the prairies, and winters up in the mountains were equally severe, bringing all mining and building activities to a halt until the spring thaw. Christmas decorations were basic—shapes cut from paper, popcorn, and dried cranberries and apple slices tied together on a thread. Children would be very lucky to receive a manufactured toy and were more likely to receive something homemade such as, for a girl, a doll made from a corn husk, animal hair, and some old cloth. A boy could expect something practical like a knife or a carved tool.

❄ ❄ ❄ ❄

CHRISTMAS, A TOWN IN ORANGE County, Florida, is themed on the festive day from which it took its name. Among the attractions at the town's Jungle Adventures recreation park is a **200-foot-long replica of an alligator**. Christmas is just one of several places with names that recall the winter holiday season. In Alaska, you will find the town of North Pole; in Georgia and Indiana, there are towns called Santa Claus; Noel in Missouri; Rudolph in Wisconsin; Snowflake in Arizona; and Dasher in Georgia.

❄ ❄ ❄ ❄

SINCE 1864 MEMBERS OF THE SERPENTINE SWIMMING CLUB HAVE MET in London's Hyde Park every Christmas morning to **race across the icy lake**. For forty years the winner of the 100-yard dash was awarded a gold medal, but in 1904 writer Sir James Barrie, a patron of the race, presented the first Peter Pan Cup, which was named after his most famous character.

"SILENT NIGHT," THE world's most popular carol, was supposedly dashed off in a couple of hours by Austrian priest Joseph Mohr. The legend goes that a few hours before Mohr was due to conduct Midnight Mass, the organ at St. Nicholas's Church in the Alpine village of Oberndorf broke down. Mohr

hastily set about writing a three-stanza carol that could be sung with just a choir or a guitar, and later that evening the strains of *"Stille Nacht"* were heard for the first time.

❄   ❄   ❄   ❄

*We consider Christmas as the encounter, the great encounter, the historical encounter, the decisive encounter, between God and mankind. He who has faith knows this truly; let him rejoice.*

POPE PAUL VI (1897–1978)

❄   ❄   ❄   ❄

*There is a remarkable breakdown of taste and intelligence at Christmas-time. Mature, responsible grown men wear neckties made of holly leaves and drink alcoholic beverages with raw egg yolks and cottage cheese in them.*

P. J. O'ROURKE (1947– )
American humorist

41

# THE SURGEON

THE ROADS WERE VERY QUIET WHEN I DROVE BACK TO QUEEN Alexandra Hospital in Portsmouth on Christmas morning to check on a patient I had operated on 12 hours earlier. I imagined I would only be there for a short while, and would be back in time to join my family for the church service up in the little chapel across the fields.

After parking the car, I decided to take the short cut up to the ward through the ER. I remember feeling a little self-conscious as I walked through the doors because I was wearing my new Christmas sweater. It all seemed very quiet, almost eerie. As I strode through I noticed someone having cardiac massage in "resuss" (the resuscitation area). For some reason, it struck me as quite a surreal sight, perhaps because this battle for life was taking place in an otherwise very still and very quiet atmosphere. Usually, the ER is a bustle of noise and activity.

As I walked into the main workstation area, there were two surgical registrars talking together, which is not something you expect to see early on Christmas morning. I knew something was up because they were both accountable to me, and my first thought was that there had been some complications with the patient on whom I'd operated the night before.

"Ah, Mr. Pemberton, we were just trying to call you," one of them said. "We might have a ruptured aortic aneurysm for you. Did you see that man in the ER?"

I was a little surprised to hear this, skeptical even, because it's very rare that someone who suffers such a rupture survives long enough for cardiac massage to be performed.

I went straight back to resuss, and the patient was looking pretty grim as the cardiac team continued to work on him. Whenever they stopped he had no blood pressure, and the consensus was that he was too far gone to be saved. Any further efforts seemed futile, so once we had established that as a certainty I turned to his wife to explain what was happening and give her the bad news. It felt very odd. A minute or two earlier I had been whistling my way across the parking lot, looking forward to having a chat with the patients on the wards, and the next thing I knew I was telling a woman her husband was about to die. "Hello, I'm the duty vascular surgeon," I heard myself say. "Your husband is having cardiac massage." I explained to her as best I could what a ruptured aneurysm meant and then said: "It seems highly likely he's about to die, whatever we do, and these are the options: though his chances of survival are very slim indeed we can take him to the operating room, or we can accept that unfortunately he's too far gone and sadly we have missed the very small window of opportunity we had to save him."

"I want you to try and save him, even if it seems impossible," she replied. Seconds later I was tearing off my Christmas sweater and quickly putting on my surgical clothes. We all rushed into the operating room, even though I was expecting someone to come in at any moment to tell me that the patient had passed away. I was absolutely stunned when he was wheeled in and I was told he still had a pulse, albeit a weak one.

We covered his chest in antiseptic and, no more than two or three minutes after talking to his wife, I was cutting the man open from his sternum to his pubis and clamping his aorta just above the diseased segment that had burst. That done, there was a brief respite while the anesthetic team improved his general condition by giving him more fluids and stabilizing his blood pressure. This is a great moment because if the patient's still alive when you clamp them, you know they're in with a chance. We had to use an awful lot of blood throughout the operation because, as is the case with patients in shock, his blood wouldn't clot and everything we stitched just carried on bleeding until the coagulant products eventually started to work their magic. The human body contains an average of eight units of blood, and we used about 30 in this operation, which is masses.

We spent a full four hours repairing the rupture but as the operation wore on I grew in confidence that he was going to make it. It was an exciting feeling, knowing that this man was coming back from the brink. Somehow, the fact that it was Christmas Day made it all the more thrilling.

It was the middle of the afternoon by the time we were done and the man could be wheeled out of the operating room to one of the wards. I was still buzzing with excitement when I finally arrived home—just in time to carve the giant turkey and pour the wine for our guests. In the event, our man made a full recovery, was back home two weeks later, and at the time of writing he's still alive, over four years later. It wasn't quite a miracle, but it wasn't far off. Not since I was a young child have I felt the spirit of Christmas so keenly as I did that day in 2002.

MARK PEMBERTON, vascular surgeon

# Reindeer Sausages and Minced Coffins

## Christmas Food and Drink

*Take 40 eggs and divide the whites from the yolks & beat them to a froth then work 4 pounds of butter to a cream & put the whites of eggs to it a Spoon full at a time till it is well work'd then put 4 pounds of sugar finely powderd [sic] to it in the same manner then put in the Youlks [sic] of eggs & 5 pounds of flower [sic] & 5 pounds of fruit. 2 hours will bake it add to it half an ounce of mace & nutmeg half a pint of wine & some frensh [sic] brandy.*

TRADITIONAL CHRISTMAS FRUITCAKE RECIPE
found among papers of Martha Washington,
wife of First U.S. President George Washington

✳ ✳ ✳ ✳

*A merry Christmas and a happy New Year,*
*Your pockets full of money and your cellar full of beer.*

OLD SAYING

✳ ✳ ✳ ✳

*Men may talk of country Christmases*
*Their thirty pound butter'd eggs,*
*Their pies of carps' tongues,*
*Their pheasants drench'd with ambergris:*
*The carcases of three fat wethers bruised for gravy;*
*To make sauce for a single peacock;*
*Yet their feasts were fasts*
*Compared with the city's.*

PHILIP MASSINGER (1583–1640), English dramatist
*The City Madam*

## To Roast a Turkey

*In very cold weather a turkey in its feathers will hang (in an airy larder)
quite a fortnight with advantage; and, however fine a quality of bird it may
be, unless sufficiently long kept, it will prove not worth the dressing, though it
should always be perfectly sweet when prepared for table…. Pluck, draw and
singe it with exceeding care; wash and then dry it thoroughly with clean cloths,
or merely wipe the outside well, without wetting it, and pour water plentifully
through the inside. Fill the beast with forcemeat [a kind of stuffing], or with the
finest sausage meat, highly seasoned with minced herbs, lemon-rind, mace and
cayenne. Truss the bird firmly, lay it to a clear sound fire, baste it constantly and
bountifully with butter and serve it when done with good brown gravy and well-
made bread sauce. An entire chain of delicate fried sausages is still often placed in
the dish, round a turkey, as a garnish…. A turkey should be laid at first far from
the fire, and drawn nearer when half done though never sufficiently so to scorch
it; it should be as well roasted, for even the most inveterate advocates of under
dressed meat will seldom tolerate the taste or the sight of partially raw poultry.*

ELIZA ACTON (1799–1859), English cook
*Modern Cookery for Private Families,* first published 1845

❄ ❄ ❄ ❄

### Necessary Amount of Food

*In estimating the amount of food to be taken by a healthy man during the twenty-
four hours [of Christmas Day], it has to be considered whether the person has
work to perform, or if he will remain at rest; also if he has to work, whether his
brain or muscles are to be employed. It has been proved by experience that the
harder the work performed, the more food is required to replace the tissues worn
away by the exertion. Food that contains much nitrogen is best suited for those
who work by muscular exertion, while individuals who have to undergo much
mental exertion, and thus wear away the tissues of the brain and nervous system,
require principally food in which the phosphates are most abundant.*

*Cassell's Book of the Household,* 1878

❄ ❄ ❄ ❄

IN 1819 COOKS IN DEVON, ENGLAND, PRODUCED A
**Christmas pudding** weighing 900 pounds.

*Christmas, n. A day set apart and consecrated to gluttony, drunkenness, maudlin sentiment, gift-taking, public dullness and domestic behavior.*

AMBROSE BIERCE (1842–1914), American writer
*The Devil's Dictionary*

❋ ❋ ❋ ❋

*To three pound of flour, sprinkle a tea cup of fine powdered coriander seed, rub in one pound of butter, and one and a half pound sugar, dissolve one tea spoonful of pearlash [a rising agent] in a tea cup of milk, kneed all together well, roll three quarters of an inch thick, and cut or stamp into shape and slice as you please, bake slowly fifteen or twenty minutes; tho' hard and dry at first, if put in an earthen pot, and dry cellar, or damp room, they will be finer, softer and better when six months old.*

CHRISTMAS COOKEY RECIPE
from *American Cookery* by Amelia Simmons (1796),
acknowledged to be the first American cookbook

❋ ❋ ❋ ❋

THE NAME "TURKEY" IS THOUGHT TO HAVE BEEN GIVEN TO THE BIRD after a misunderstanding about its native habitat. The birds come from Mexico originally, but when they first arrived in England in the sixteenth century they were brought by sailors from the eastern Mediterranean known as "Turkey merchants." The English weren't the only people unsure about the strange-looking bird's origins. Most Europeans were under the impression it came from India, a confusion arising out of the newly discovered regions of the Caribbean and Central America, known as the Spanish Indies or the New Indies.

❋ ❋ ❋ ❋

*Oysters on Half Shell, Game Soup, Boiled White Fish, Sauce Maitre d'Hotel, Roast Goose, Apple Sauce, Boiled Potatoes, Mashed Turnips, Creamed Parsnips, Stewed Onions, Boiled Rice, Lobster Salad, Canvas Back Duck, Christmas Plum Pudding, Sauce, Vanilla Ice cream, Mince Pie, Orange Jelly, Delicate Cake, Salted Almonds, Confectionery, Fruits, Coffee.*

SUGGESTED CHRISTMAS DAY DINNER MENU
from *The White House Cook Book*,
by Mrs. F. L. Gillette and Hugo Ziemann, 1903

## Great Slaughter at Louth

*On Friday week, Mr. Valentine Fell, poulterer, of Louth, near Boston, assisted by forty-five persons, commenced his annual slaughtering of poultry for the Christmas market. No fewer than 4,000 geese ... as well as 1,500 ducks, turkeys, and fowls, comprised the number to be slaughtered. They were all consigned to Leadenhall market, and were calculated to weigh upwards of thirty tons. Many of the geese were of remarkably large kind, and weighed from 16lb to 20lb.*

*Illustrated London News,* December 22, 1849

*To Arrange a Christmas Dinner: Place a high pyramid of evergreens . . . in the centre of the table. Let a roasted turkey of uncommon size occupy the middle or centre of one side of the table, on one end let there be a cold boiled ham, and at the other, fricasseed chicken or a roast pig; with the turkey serve mashed potatoes and turnips, boiled onions and dressed celery, or other salad with apple sauce—near the ham place fried or mashed potatoes and pickles or mangoes: and with the pig or fricassee, the same as with the turkey; large pitchers of sweet cider (or where that is not desired, ice water) should be placed diagonally opposite each other, on two corners of the table; boiled turkey with oyster sauce may occupy the place of the fricassee, or instead, a fine oyster pie. For desert, there should be only two very large and ornamental mince pies, one sufficiently large that each of the company may be helped from it, in token of common interest, is desirable. Ice creams and jellies and jams and ripe fruits and nuts, with sweet cider and syrup water of different sorts, or wines, complete the dessert. Biscuit and jelly sandwich may be served at dessert, or paste puffs and charlotte de russe or blancmange with strands of jelly.*

*Mrs. Crowen's American Lady's Cookery Book,* 1847

❄ ❄ ❄ ❄

THE TURKEY WAS ORIGINALLY KNOWN IN PARTS OF FRANCE AS A *jésuite*, after the Jesuit monastic order who brought the birds home from their **missionary endeavors** in Central America.

*A noble dish is a turkey, roast or boiled. A Christmas dinner, with the middle classes of this empire, would scarcely be a Christmas dinner without its turkey; and we can hardly imagine an object of greater envy than is presented by a respected portly pater-familias carving, at the season devoted to good cheer and genial charity, his own fat turkey, and carving it well.*

*The only art consists, as in the carving of a goose, in getting from the breast as many fine slices as possible; and all must have remarked the very great difference in the large number of people whom a good carver will find slices for, and the comparatively few that a bad carver will succeed in serving. As we have stated in both the carving of a duck and goose, the carver should commence cutting slices close to the wing and then proceed upwards towards the ridge of the breastbone: this is not the usual plan, but, in practice, will be found the best.*

*The breast is the only part which is looked on as fine in a turkey, the legs being very seldom cut off and eaten at table: they are usually removed to the kitchen, where they are taken off, to appear only in a form which seems to have a special attraction at a bachelor's supper-table, we mean devilled: served in this way, they are especially liked and relished.*

*A boiled turkey is carved in the same manner as when roasted.*

MRS. BEETON (1836–1865), British cookery writer
*Book of Household Management*

*... Meanwhile, it remains true that I shall eat a great deal of turkey this Christmas; and it is not in the least true (as the vegetarians say) that I shall do it because I do not realise what I am doing, or because I do what I know is wrong, or that I do it with shame or doubt or a fundamental unrest of conscience. In one sense I know quite well what I am doing; in another sense I know quite well that I know not what I do. Scrooge and the Cratchits and I are, as I have said, all in one boat; the turkey and I are, to say the most of it, ships that pass in the night, and greet each other in passing. I wish him well; but it is really practically impossible to discover whether I treat him well. I can avoid, and I do avoid with horror, all special and artificial tormenting of him, sticking pins in him for fun or sticking knives in him for scientific investigation. But whether by feeding him*

*slowly and killing him quickly for the needs of my brethren, I have improved in his own solemn eyes his own strange and separate destiny, whether I have made him in the sight of God a slave or a martyr, or one whom the gods love and who die young—that is far more removed from my possibilities of knowledge than the most abstruse intricacies of mysticism or theology. A turkey is more occult and awful than all the angels and archangels in so far as God has partly revealed to us an angelic world, he has partly told us what an angel means. But God has never told us what a turkey means. And if you go and stare at a live turkey for an hour or two, you will find by the end of it that the enigma has rather increased than diminished.*

G. K. CHESTERTON (1874–1936), English writer
*All Things Considered: Christmas*

❄ ❄ ❄ ❄

Two centuries ago every well-to-do family made a
Christmas pie or shred pie: "a most learned mixture
of neats' tongues, chickens, eggs,
sugar, raisins etc...." They ought
to be confined to the season of
Christmas. No modern receipts
[recipes] are similar and the less
meat they contain the better.
*Cassell's Book of the Household.* 1878

❄ ❄ ❄ ❄

EGGS

A CHRISTMAS PUDDING IN THE MIDDLE
Ages took the form of spicy porridge known
as "frumenty." The dish was considered a
tremendous treat, even by overindulged royals
and noblemen, already at bursting point after a week of feasting
on peacocks, oxen, swans, boars, and small pheasants. It consisted
mainly of **cracked wheat boiled in animal stock** and mixed with egg
yolks and threads of the highly prized spice saffron. Recipes differed
from region to region and household to household but most came to
include sweeter spices like cinnamon and nutmeg, as well as currants
and other dried fruit. The mixture was left to set before being
served, often as an accompaniment to meat dishes.

The turkey is undoubtedly one of the handsomest presents which the New World has offered to the Old. . . . In the course of my researches I also discovered that the acclimitization of the species in France was a gradual process. Enlightened students of the subject have informed that about the middle of the last century, out of every twenty turkeys hatched, not more than ten grew to maturity; whereas today, all things being equal, the proportion is fifteen to twenty. Rain-storms are particularly fatal to them. The heavy rain-drops, driven by the wind, beat upon their soft and unprotected skulls and kill them.

JEAN ANTHELME BRILLAT-SAVARIN (1755–1826), politician and gastronome
*The Philosopher in the Kitchen*, 1825

❄ ❄ ❄ ❄

## A dog isn't just for Christmas. It's jolly nice cold on the 26th too.

ENGLISH SAYING

❄ ❄ ❄ ❄

So coming to Calas [Calais] the next day it was Christmas Day and the first Christmas Day ever I had out of England, but not the last by a great many. We had but small Christmas cheer, not having Christmas pie or roast beef, or plum podich and suchlike, I remember that the poorest people in England would have a bit of something that was good on such a day, and that many beggars would fare much better than we did: for we had nothing but a little bit of Irish beef for four men, which had lain in pickle two or three years and was rusty as the devil, with a little stinking oil or butter, which was all colours of the rainbow, many men in England greasing their cartwheels with better: and also we had not two or three days to play in and go where we would, as the worst servants had in England, but as soon as we had ate our large dinner, which was done in three or four mouthfuls, we must work all the day after, and maybe a great part of the night.

SEAMAN JOHN BARLOW
*Journal*, Christmas 1661

❄ ❄ ❄ ❄

A WARNING TO VIRGIN CHRISTMAS **duck-eaters**: the bones of a duck are much heavier than those of a turkey or chicken, so you need a bigger bird to get the same amount of meat.

SALES OF GOOSE FAT HAVE SKYROCKETED IN RECENT YEARS AFTER
several television chefs championed this once-common food item.
Used in the past as a hand cream and a treatment for chilblains, the
fat is superb for frying eggs and roasting potatoes, owing to the very
high temperatures it can reach without burning.

# CHRISTMAS DINNER TIPS

*If you've drawn the short straw
and have been elected to remove
the innards of your fresh turkey,
be careful with its gall bladder,
that nasty-looking little green sack
attached to the liver. If it bursts, the
bile will seep into the meat and give
it a very unhealthy appearance.*

*Pan fry the liver and eat it on toast,
like hot pâté.*

*Get rid of feathery tufts by passing
the bird over an open flame.*

*Stuffing turkey may be traditional
but it slows up the cooking time,
and makes the bird more susceptible
to drying out. If you do stuff it,
you will have to baste the bird at
regular intervals to keep the moisture
in. Better, then, to make stuffing
separately and put onions and lemon
halves in the cavity and pour some
water into the bottom of the foil.
This will improve the flavor and keep
it moist.*

*For the best flavor and texture, cook
the turkey upside down so that all
juices run into the white meat. It
looks weird, but then turkeys don't*

*exactly look handsome or "normal"
at the best of times, alive or dead.*

*It's easier to carve a turkey if you
take its legs off first.*

*If your gravy is too thin, just make a
quick paste of butter and flour and
stir it in.*

*To remove the excess fat from gravy,
let it cool a little and then drop in
a couple of ice cubes. The fat will
congeal more quickly, allowing you
to lift it out more easily.*

*You can extract the natural sweetness
of carrots, onions, and parsnips by
adding a sprinkle of sugar while they
cook. A big nob of butter will give
them a fine glaze.*

## Christmas Dinner Shortcuts

* For a quick alternative to roasted or boiled root vegetables, make them into a gratin by slicing them thinly and covering each layer with a mixture of milk, cream, nutmeg, and whole grain mustard, adding slices of garlic and onions to concentrate the flavor.

* Make the cranberry sauce and prepare and peel potatoes and other vegetables the day before.

* It will be several days before you can get your hands on the turkey bones to make a stock as you work your way through the carcass of meat. But you can make an instant stock as follows: put the turkey giblets into a bowl with an onion, a carrot, water, and seasoning and then heat in the microwave until it's done (roughly 10 to 15 minutes).

* Improve cheap crackers by slipping extra gifts in through the ends (such as good chocolates, etc.).

❄ ❄ ❄ ❄

## Typical Swedish Smörgåsbord on Christmas Day

Christmas ham, pork sausage, herring salad, pickled herring, homemade liver pâté, egg and anchovy mix (*gubbröra*), flavored rye bread (*vörtbröd*), potatoes, and a special fish dish called *lutfisk*. The ham is boiled, then basted with a mixture of egg, bread crumbs, and mustard before it is grilled for a glazed effect. *Lutfisk* is dried whitefish soaked in water and lye so that it swells before it is cooked.

❄ ❄ ❄ ❄

*Christmas is a season of such infinite labour, as well as expense in the shopping and present-making line, that almost every woman I know is good for nothing in purse and person for a month afterwards, done up physically, and broken down financially.*

FANNY KEMBLE (1809–1893), British actress and author

* An Assortment of Artisanal and Local Cheeses served with a Bountiful Display of Crackers, Winter Fruits, and Spiced Nuts

* Chilled Gulf Shrimp Cocktail served with Cocktail Sauce and Remoulade

* Bourbon-Glazed Virginia Ham served with Cheesy Stone-Ground Grits

* Crispy Chicken-Fried Steak Fingers with Creamed Pan Drippings

* Roasted Lamb Chops with Rosemary Sea Salt with Mission Fig Chutney and Mint Jelly

* Fruitwood Smoked Copper River Salmon served with Fresh Potato Pancakes and Traditional Garnitures

* Maryland Crab Cakes with Lemon Caper Sauce

* Orzo Salad with Roasted Artichokes, Tomatoes, and Olives with Feta Cheese Vinaigrette

* Homemade Tamales with Roasted Poblanos and Vidalia Onions with Black Beans and Tomatillo Sauce

* White and Green Asparagus and French Green Bean Tier with Garlic Aioli

**Menu for the 2007 Holiday Receptions at the White House**

*The tradition of the Christmas candy cane is thought to have come to North America with German settlers in the eighteenth and nineteenth centuries. Originally the hard candy came as a white stick and it was only at the start of the twentieth century that manufacturers added the distinctive red stripes and the crook-shaped twist at the top. A popular myth is that a choirmaster at Cologne Cathedral in Germany, back in the 1600s, was the first to bend the canes into the shape of a shepherd's staff to distribute among children after Festive period church services. The truth, however, is probably more prosaic: manufacturers came up with the idea as a practical way of encouraging consumers to display them on their trees.*

❅ ❅ ❅ ❅

LATE DECEMBER WAS A LOGICAL TIME OF YEAR FOR our ancestors to have a feast, being the season when food harvested in the autumn needed finishing up before it succumbed to decay, and animals that struggle for food in winter were slaughtered. It was also the time when beers and wines, made in the autumn, were **mature enough to drink**. Pigs were often killed at the year's end because they had scoffed most of the beechnuts and acorns that autumn had strewn for them over the woodland floor. For centuries pigs and boars formed the focus of the Christmas feast in northern European cultures.

LOVERS OF BRUSSELS SPROUTS SAY THE REASON THE REST OF US loathe them comes down to the fact that we don't know how to cook them properly. Invariably they are overdone, which removes the sweetness, but cooked properly, this much-libeled vegetable possesses a delicate flavor. Overcooking releases sulphur compounds in the sprouts, creating the vegetable's characteristic farty aroma. Steaming, rather than boiling them, helps to preserve their sweetness. Some claim Brussels sprouts are better in late winter after they have enjoyed the benefit of a **few sharp frosts**.

* * * *

*Not drunk is he who from the floor*
*Can rise alone and still drink more*
*But drunk is he who prostrate lies,*
*Without the power to drink and rise.*

THOMAS LOVE PEACOCK (1785–1866)
*The Misfortunes of Elphin,* 1829

* * * *

THE FIRST WRITTEN REFERENCE TO BRUSSELS SPROUTS IS found in 1587, and they became known as Brussels sprouts because of their **great popularity in Belgium**.

* * * *

CUTTING A CROSS ON THE BASE OF A BRUSSELS SPROUT IS AN OLD English custom performed partly out of a belief that the inside will then cook at the same rate as the outside, but also out of the superstition that it will **keep out the devil**. (Our ancestors were quick to accuse vegetables of consorting with Satan. Broad beans, in particular, came under heavy suspicion for many centuries, probably as a result of the vegetables' tendency to cause unsettled sleep if eaten late in the evening.) Today, most cooks contest that "crossing" lets the flavor escape and should thus be avoided. Driving home their point, "anti-crossers" will also tell you that the practice loosens the leaves and may even lead to the total disintegration of the vegetable.

A TURTLE ENJOYING A SPECIAL
Christmas meal of Brussels sprouts
triggered a Boxing Day emergency
in 2006 when it set off an alarm
at an aquatic center in Weymouth,
England—by **passing wind**. The
fart bubbles rose to the surface of
the turtle's water tank where they
popped and splashed water on to
an alarm sensor, bringing the local
fire crews rushing to the scene in
a blare of sirens and flashing blue
lights.

❄   ❄   ❄   ❄

FOR A HUMBLE PIECE OF PASTRY FILLED WITH NOTHING MORE
than dried fruit, nuts, and suet, the mince pie has suffered a
remarkably controversial reputation on both sides of the Atlantic.
Mince pies originated in England where they were once made with
real meat and were sometimes known as "coffins" because they
were rectangular in shape. Sometimes they were made to look like
Jesus' manger with a pastry baby stuck on top, which didn't go
down very well with the English Puritans nor the first Pilgrims to
settle in America. Both groups being great despisers of idolatry
and frivolity, they condemned the crib-shaped pastries as popish
works of the devil. When Christmas reemerged in England with
the restoration of the monarchy in the 1660s, the mince pie had
become round, with no baby on top. It took the Americans a
little longer to forgive the evil pastry, and it still is not a common
feature on Christmas tables, even though many other festive
British traditions have been absorbed into the culture.

*A curious feature of an American Christmas is the eggnog and free lunch, distributed at all the hotels and cafés. A week at least before the 25th fanciful signs are suspended over the fountains of the bars (the hotel keepers are quite classic in their ideas) announcing superb lunch eggnogs on Christmas Day. . . . At the head of the [hotel] table a vast bowl ornamented with indescribable Chinese figures contains the egg-nog—a palatable compound of milk, eggs, brandy, and spices. . . . Over the eggnog mine host usually officiates, all smiles and benignity, pouring the rich draught with miraculous dexterity into cut-glass goblets, and passing it to the surrounded guests with profuse hand. On this occasion the long range of fancy drinks are forgotten. Sherry-cobblers, mint-juleps, gin-slings, and punches are set aside in order that the sway of the Christmas draught may be supreme. Free lunches are extremely common in the United States, what are called "eleven o'clock snacks" especially; but the accompaniment of egg-nog belongs unequivocally to the death of the year.*

W. F. DAWSON, *Christmas in America*, 1902

❄ ❄ ❄ ❄

ONE OF THE REASONS THE TURKEY SUPPLANTED THE GOOSE AS the main Christmas dish was its great size. Middle-class families had grown larger in Victorian times, and wider family gatherings were made possible by improved transport. One large turkey was capable of feeding a dozen or more diners. Owing to the bird's breeding habits, geese were also tougher and less appetizing than the succulent and novel turkey. Once, most geese were born in the spring and eaten young in the late summer or early autumn after they had been fattened in the freshly harvested cornfields. This was also the time of year when, happily, apples and chestnuts—fine accompaniments to goose—were in season. By Christmas, though, the goose had become a **tough old bird**, especially the ones who had spent weeks walking from East Anglia to their festive slaughter in London. Today, farmers are able to engineer breeding times so that the birds that appear at Christmas are much younger and tastier. The principle still holds good that the smaller the bird, the younger and more tender it will be.

HUGE SAVORY PIES, STUFFED WITH EVERY MANNER OF BEAST AND BIRD, used to be a commonplace sight in British households. It's strange that they have gone out of fashion, or at best have been reduced to pathetic little parcels. One of the savory pie's great virtues is that it will keep for some time when refrigerated. It is delicious eaten cold with pickles and a salad. Below is a recipe for a truly sumptuous Yorkshire Christmas pie from the great Charles Elme Francatelli, an Anglo-Italian cook who rose from humble origins to become Queen Victoria's chef. It is taken from his excellent book *A Modern Cook*, published in 1845. In 1861, he produced another classic, *A Plain Cookery Book for the Working Classes*, in which, like Jamie Oliver today, he sought to persuade ordinary people of the benefits of wholesome, healthy cooking.

*First, bone a turkey, a goose, a brace of young pheasants, four partridges, four woodcocks, a dozen snipes, four grouse, and four widgeons; then boil and trim a small York ham and two tongues. Season and garnish the inside of the fore-named game and poultry with long fillets of fat bacon and tongue, and French truffles; each must be carefully sewn up with a needle and small twine, so as to prevent the force-meat from escaping while they are being baked. When the whole of these are ready, line two round or oval braizing-pans with thin layers of fat bacon, and after the birds have been arranged therein in neat order, and covered in with layers of bacon and buttered paper, put the lids on, and set them in the oven to bake rather slowly, for about four hours: then withdraw them, and allow them to cool.*

*While the foregoing is in progress, prepare some highly-seasoned aspic-jelly with the carcasses of the game and poultry, to which add six calves' feet, and the usual complement of vegetables, &c., and when done, let it be clarified: one-half should be reduced previously to its being poured into the pie when it is baked.*

*Make about sixteen pounds of hot-water-paste, and use it to raise a pie of sufficient dimensions to admit of its holding the game and poultry prepared for the purpose.... The inside of the pie must first be lined with thin layers of fat bacon, over which spread a coating of well-seasoned force-meat of fat; the birds should then be placed in the following order: First, put the goose at the bottom with some of the small birds round it, filling up the cavities with some*

of the force-meat; then, put the turkey and the pheasants with thick slices of the boiled ham between them, reserving the woodcocks and widgeons, that these may be placed on the top: fill the cavities with force-meat and truffles, and cover the whole with thin layers of fat bacon, run a little plain melted butter over the surface, cover the pie in the usual manner, and ornament it with a bold design. The pie must now be baked, for about six hours, in an oven moderately heated, and when taken out, and after the reduced aspic above alluded to has been poured into it, stop the hole up with a small piece of paste, and set it aside in the larder to become cold.

*NOTE:* The quantity of game, &c., recommended to be used in the preparation of the foregoing pie may appear extravagant enough, but it is to be remembered that these very large pies are mostly in request at Christmas time.

Their substantial aspect renders them worthy of appearing on the side-table of those wealthy epicures who are wont to keep up the good old English style, at this season of hospitality and good cheer.

❄ ❄ ❄ ❄

FROM THE MID-1850s, WHILE MORE AND MORE WELL-TO-DO Victorians began to treat the Christmas period as a time of holiday, many **shopkeepers and tradesmen continued to work**. As a gesture of seasonal goodwill, the local baker, who had to keep his fires burning continuously, was often in the habit of letting the poor people in his neighborhood cook their Christmas geese in his huge ovens.

❄ ❄ ❄ ❄

*There never was such a goose. Bob said he didn't believe there ever was such a goose cooked. Its tenderness and flavour, size and cheapness, were the themes of universal admiration. Eked out by apple-sauce and mashed potatoes, it was a sufficient dinner for the whole family; indeed, as Mrs. Cratchit said with great delight (surveying one small atom of a bone upon the dish), they hadn't ate it all at last! Yet every one had had enough, and the youngest Cratchits in particular, were steeped in sage and onion to the eyebrows!*

CHARLES DICKENS
*A Christmas Carol,* 1843

AS IF SHE DIDN'T HAVE ENOUGH ON HER PLATE ALREADY, CELEBRITY chef Nigella Lawson has taken time to come up with a brilliant plan to increase the **juiciness** of Christmas turkeys. All you need is a large bucket, or a small tub, lots of water, a cupboard full of spices and other goodies—and a memo stuck on the fridge to remind you to prepare it all 48 hours before you plan to put the turkey in the oven. In her book *Feast*, Nigella produces a list of perfect ingredients to add to the water, but I'm sure it wouldn't be a disaster if you were missing a few of them or opted to substitute some with similar alternatives. Once you have submerged the turkey, leave it outside, or somewhere cold, and make sure you cover it with something heavy—unless you want every predator in the neighborhood dropping by for a snack. Take it out an hour before cooking, and dry it. Nigella suggests the following: for 6 quarts of water, add 2½ cups salt, 3 tbsp peppercorns, a bouquet garni, 2 tbsp white mustard seeds, 2 cups superfine sugar, 2 peeled and quartered onions, a slice of ginger, 1 cinnamon stick, 1 tbsp caraway seeds, 4 cloves, 2 tbsp allspice berries, 4 star anise, 1 orange, 4 tbsp maple syrup, 4 tbsp runny honey, and some parsley stalks.

*Mince pies are not healthful, and one batch in a season is quite sufficient. A shin of beef boiled down till very tender, one pound of nice clear beef suet chopped very fine, a table-spoonful of salt, six pounds of greening apples peeled, cored and chopped, three pounds of raisins stoned, three of currants carefully cleaned, one pound of brown sugar, a cup of maple syrup, half a pound of citron, shredded, half a pound of candied lemon peel, a quart of the best cider. This mixture makes rich pies, but mince pies are nothing if not rich. These are also particularly fine in flavor. Instead of cider, some persons put in a quart of Madeira wine, and a little brandy; but it is better not to use alcohol in food when it can be avoided.*

Jennie June's American Cookery Book, 1870

*A great deal of steam! The pudding was out of the copper. A smell like a washing-day! That was the cloth! A smell like an eating-house and a pastry cook's next door to each other, with a laundress's next door to that! That was the pudding. In half a minute, Mrs. Cratchit entered—flushed, but smiling proudly—with the pudding, like a speckled cannon-ball, so hard and firm, blazing in half-a-quartern of ignited brandy, and bedight with Christmas holly stuck into the top. Oh, a wonderful pudding. Bob Cratchit said, and calmly too, that he regarded it as the greatest success achieved by Mrs. Cratchit since their marriage. Mrs. Cratchit said that now the weight was off her mind, she would confess she had had her doubts about the quantity of flour.*

CHARLES DICKENS
*A Christmas Carol,* 1843

## DRUNK CHRISTMAS CAKE

1 pint water
1 cup sugar
4 large eggs
2 cups dried fruit
1 tsp salt
1 cup demerara sugar
3 cups nuts
2 tbsp lemon juice
1 orange rind
1 very large bottle of whisky

*Try the whisky to check for good quality. Find a large bowl. Check the whisky again to make sure it hasn't gone bad in the meantime. Just to be extra sure, pour a proper glass of it and drink. Repeat until absolutely certain. Turn on the food professor, and beat up the butter in the large bowl. Add sugar and beat the buffer again. Check the whisky is still room temperature. Turn up the volume on the processor. Lob the five beggs into the bowl and chuck in the fup of cried druit. Mix on the whizzy turner thing. If the fired druit gets stuck in the food professor's blades, lisdodge the gunk. Sample the whisky to check no one has sneaked in and diluted it. Next, the salt. Or whatever. Make sure whisky is still smooth to the tongue. Now shit the lemon juice and strain your nuts. Add one table of lemon. Do the sugar or something. Whatever's to hand. Wash down the oven. Turn the cake tin to 450 degrees. Burn off the food professor. Drop the bowl on the floor, go to bed taking care to bring whisky bottle with you in case it falls into wrong hands. Lie down and enjoy a warm glow of satisfaction at a job well done.*

*Ha più da fare che i forni di Natale in Inghilterra.*

("He has more to do than the ovens in England at Christmas.")

ITALIAN PROVERB

❄ ❄ ❄ ❄

*To make up for the shortage of shell eggs, there will be a double ration of dried eggs. Between now and Christmas there will be an acute shortage of fruit. There are practically no apples on the market, and it is doubtful if many children will get oranges. The sale of nuts is practically non-existent. For those who may be eating in restaurants during Christmas there should be plenty of fish.... British troops on duty in Home Commands will have an egg with their bacon for breakfast; roast pork or poultry, potatoes, sprouts and Christmas pudding for dinner; while teatime will bring cake and mince pies.*

*News of the World,*
December 19, 1943

❄ ❄ ❄ ❄

REINDEER MEAT IS VERY POPULAR in the Scandinavian countries and among other people living close to the Arctic Circle. The Lapps serve **smoked roast reindeer** in thin slices and in sandwiches. They also serve it sautéed as a main dish. The meat has a mild gamy flavor and is packed with goodness, partly because of the good food the animal eats, including "reindeer moss," which is packed with vitamin C. Reindeer meatballs are sold in cans in Alaska, and reindeer sausages are a common sight in local stores.

❄ ❄ ❄ ❄

*A man might then behold
At Christmas, in each hall
Good fires to curb the cold,
And meat for great and small.
The neighbours were
friendly bidden,
And all had welcome true,
The poor from the gates
were not chidden,
When this old cap was new.*

OLD ENGLISH SONG

❄ ❄ ❄ ❄

*Our [Christmas Day] breakfast consisted of what the Squire denominated true old English fare. He indulged in some bitter lamentations over modern breakfasts of tea-and-toast, which he censured as among the causes of modern effeminacy and weak nerves, and* the decline of old English heartiness; and though he admitted them to his table to suit the palates of his guests, yet there was a brave display of cold meats, wine, and ale, on the sideboard.

WASHINGTON IRVING
*The Sketch Book,*
1819–1820

IN A 1784 LETTER TO HIS daughter, Benjamin Franklin, one of the Founding Fathers of the United States of America, lamented that the turkey had not been chosen ahead of the eagle as the country's official bird. The following is an excerpt from the letter:

*For my own part I wish the Bald Eagle had not been chosen the Representative of our Country. He is a Bird of bad moral Character. He does not get his Living honestly. You may have seen him perched on some dead Tree near the River, where, too lazy to fish for himself, he watches the Labour of the Fishing Hawk; and when that diligent Bird has at length taken a Fish, and is bearing it to his Nest for the Support of his Mate and young Ones, the Bald Eagle pursues him and takes it from him.*

*With all this Injustice, he is never in good Case but like those among Men who live by Sharping & Robbing he is generally poor and often very lousy. Besides he is a rank Coward: The little King Bird not bigger than a Sparrow attacks him boldly and drives him out of the District. He is therefore by no means a proper Emblem for the brave and honest Cincinnati of America who have driven all the King birds from our Country....*

*I am on this account not displeased that the Figure is not known as a Bald Eagle, but looks more like a Turkey. For in Truth the Turkey is in Comparison a much more respectable Bird, and withal a true original Native of America.... He is besides, though a little vain and silly, a Bird of Courage, and would not hesitate to attack a Grenadier of the British Guards who should presume to invade his Farm Yard with a red Coat on.*

## Turkey Facts

* The wild turkey is native to the United States but it nearly disappeared in the early 1900s due to over-hunting and woods being cleared for farmland and housing. But thanks to the efforts of conservationists, they have staged a remarkable revival and now live in over 40 states and are so numerous that hunters are allowed to shoot them again.
* Farmed turkeys are bred to gain weight quickly and the male (tom) can balloon to 30 pounds within four months of hatching. Most domestic turkeys are so big they cannot fly and the breasts of some are so great that the birds often fall over. The world's biggest turkey weighed 88 pounds.
* Turkey skins were once used to make boots and belts.
* Wild turkeys spend the night in trees, perched on branches, away from predators.

❄ ❄ ❄ ❄

## Eggnog

*To make a gallon of this eggnog will require a pound and a quarter of pulverized sugar, twelve fresh eggs, a quart of cognac, half a pint of champagne, two quarts of fresh milk, one quart of rich cream, and about a tablespoonful of powdered nutmeg. Mix these ingredients thoroughly, then incorporate with them the yolks of the dozen eggs that have been beaten to a froth. Stir persistently and steadily until the blend is perfect; pour the result into the well chilled punch bowl, and if you can procure some very old rum, add about three tablespoonfuls. Beat the white of the twelve eggs until very stiff, place this meringue on top of the eggnog, and you may feel reasonably assured that your guests will have no cause to complain about your mode of entertainment.*

New York Times, December 15, 1907

❄ ❄ ❄ ❄

RESEARCHERS IN THE NETHERLANDS RECENTLY COMPLETED A LONG investigation into the effect of a diet high in Brussels sprouts on DNA damage. Of ten healthy male volunteers, five ate a diet that included about 10 ounces of sprouts a day, while the other five ate a diet free of them and all other cruciferous vegetables. After three weeks, the sprout group showed a **28 percent decrease** in measured DNA damage. The finding was considered important because scientists believe that any reduction in DNA damage could mean a reduction in the risk of inherited forms of cancer.

THE AUSTRALIAN *WOMAN'S MIRROR*, A MAGAZINE PUBLISHED between 1924 and 1961, produced a famous recipe in 1927 called Empire Christmas Pudding, encouraging its readers to show their loyalty to the British Crown. All of its ingredients were sourced from colonies and dominions of the British Empire:

*5 lb. sultanas* (Australia)
*5 lb. currants* (Australia)
*5 lb. stoned raisins* (South Africa)
*1½ lb. minced apple* (Canada)
*5 lb. breadcrumbs* (United Kingdom)
*5 lb. beef suet* (New Zealand)
*2 lb. cut candied peel* (South Africa)
*2½ lb. flour* (United Kingdom)
*20 eggs* (Irish Free State)
*2½ lb. Demerara sugar* (West Indies)
*2 oz. ground cinnamon* (Ceylon)
*1½ oz. ground cloves* (Zanzibar)
*1½ oz. ground nutmegs* (Straits Settlements)
*1 teaspoonful pudding spice* (India)
*2 gills rum* (Jamaica)
*1 gill brandy* (Cyprus)
*2 quarts old beer* (England)

# Christmas Feast Recipes

## SIMPLE TURKEY SOUP

1 lb. chopped vegetables (carrots, leeks, swede, celery, onions) ✳ 2½ cups turkey stock ✳ Leftover turkey meat (optional) ✳ 1 large dollop of turkey dripping or butter per 1 lb. of vegetables ✳ Seasoning

Sweat the vegetables in dripping or butter in a large pan for 10 minutes over a low heat. Add stock and leave to simmer, with the lid on, lightly for 90 minutes. If you use leftover meat, add some more stock. Purée the soup, and salt and pepper if needed.

## PERFECT ROAST POTATOES

Cut large potatoes to your preferred size and parboil for about 5 minutes, then drain and shake them around the pan to roughen the surfaces. In a (hot) preheated oven, place a roasting pan containing a generous quantity of fat or oil. When it starts to smoke, take the pan out and pour in the potatoes, basting them all over before returning them to the oven. Let them cook for about an hour, turning them from time to time to ensure all sides are done equally.

## ROAST GOOSE

Roasting a goose is pretty straightforward as the bird bastes itself. It's best to drain much of the fat from the goose at the outset, otherwise it will be too greasy for all except people who live in caves. To degrease it, prick dozens of holes all over the bird, and place it on a slatted tray over a roasting pan in an oven preheated to 350°F. Leave for roughly an hour. Make sure the temperature isn't too high at any point during the roasting or the skin will blister and burn. Take the goose out and pat it all over with paper towels, inside as well, to soak up as much grease as possible. Add the stuffing of your choice (many chefs recommend a sweeter stuffing with goose, perhaps one made with cranberries and other dried fruit). Put it back in the oven in a roasting pan and let it cook for 25 minutes per pound, minus the hour it has already had to degrease it. Rebaste every half-hour using its own considerable juices.

## STIR-FRIED SPICY RED CABBAGE WITH APPLES

If you're short on time, a quick alternative to traditional braised red cabbage is to stir-fry it. One of the great features of red cabbage is that, unlike most vegetables, it is better the day after it's cooked.

½ cup butter ✳ 2 tbsp oil ✳ 1 large onion, chopped ✳
2 sweet apples, cored and chopped ✳ 3 garlic cloves, chopped
✳ 1 lb. red cabbage ✳ Generous pinches of cinnamon,
nutmeg, and cloves ✳ Seasoning to taste ✳ 1 tbsp brown sugar
✳ 1 tbsp red wine vinegar

Melt the butter and oil in a large, heavy frying pan or a wok with a heavy base. Soften the onion for a couple of minutes, then add the apple and garlic and cook for another 2 minutes. Turn up the heat and add the cabbage, stirring and turning it constantly with a wooden spoon as it fries. After a few minutes add the spices and seasoning; reduce the heat and leave it for 5 or 10 minutes, stirring occasionally. When it's virtually done, turn the heat up again before stirring in the sugar and vinegar. Stir everything thoroughly, then serve.

## CHESTNUT AND CRANBERRY STUFFING

3 cups chestnuts ✳ 2$^1$/$_2$ cups cranberries, dried or fresh ✳ 1 lb. sausage meat ✳ Zest of 1 orange ✳ Pinch of nutmeg and cinnamon

If you use fresh chestnuts, make a slight incision in their shells before placing them in a hot oven. When the shells open up, peel them off together with the first layer of the skin. Wash the chestnuts and chop them very coarsely before combining with the sausage meat, orange zest, cranberries, spices, and salt and pepper. Take all the ingredients and knead into a big gooey mess before plunging it all into the cavity of your bird.

## CRANBERRY, PORT, AND ORANGE SAUCE

1 large orange ✳ 1$^1$/$_2$ cups superfine sugar ✳ 3$^1$/$_2$ ounces port ✳ 3 cups cranberries, fresh or frozen ✳ 1 medium apple, finely chopped

Grate orange zest and squeeze the juice. Dissolve the sugar in a pan with the juice and all but a drop of the port. Add the cranberries, apple, and orange rind and cook for about 10 minutes until the mixture has softened and the juice has become stickier. Add the last dash of port.

## PROPER BRUSSELS SPROUTS

Steam the sprouts for seven to eight minutes, then toss them in butter, fresh herbs, chopped garlic, salt, and pepper. They are even better if you add some shallots and bacon that you've cooked in a neighboring frying pan.

MULLED CIDER MAKES A GOOD ALTERNATIVE TO mulled wine, especially if served after Christmas either before or with a rough-and-ready meal of leftover meats, vegetables, and pickles.

## MULLED CIDER

7 medium apples ✴ 12 whole cloves ✴ 5 pints good-quality cider ✴ 3 cinnamon sticks ✴ 1 orange ✴ 2 cups sugar ✴ ½ tsp ground ginger ✴ ½ tsp ground nutmeg

Spike six apples with cloves and bake. When they are soft, place in a large saucepan over medium heat and add the cider and all other ingredients. Bring to a boil then reduce to simmer for 30 minutes or so. Strain the mixture and serve with slices of apple and orange.

A POINSETTIA IS A FINE COCKTAIL TO SERVE AT CHRISTMAS TIME. IT'S so easy to prepare that even an idiot or a politician can make one. You wouldn't want more than a couple of them, though, unless you want to end up facedown on the rug. The cocktail is a simple mixture of dry sparkling white wine, vodka or Cointreau, and cranberry juice. Mix to taste and preferred strength.

# ∽ Christmas Leftover Recipes ∽

Roasted turkey, like chicken, is more flavorsome when reheated a day or two later. Below are some simple suggestions for using up what remains of your turkey and other Christmas foods. All the recipes are for four servings, unless otherwise stated.

## SIMPLE CORONATION TURKEY

This is a very quick and easy dish, which can be used to fill sandwiches or baked potatoes, or served as it comes with salads and cold meats. Simply take a mixing bowl, add the following and stir it around until it is well combined: chopped turkey, mayonnaise, curry powder, raisins, crumbled walnuts or almonds, chopped dried apricots, and some honey or apricot jam or mango chutney.

# CHOCAHOLIC CHRISTMAS DESSERT

14 oz. good-quality cooking chocolate * 17 oz. mixed dried fruit *
8 shortbread biscuits, crushed * Heaping tbsp butter * Generous
splash of rum or brandy

Melt the chocolate, stir in the fruit, shortbread, and melted butter
to make the mixing a little easier. Refrigerate in a tray overnight and
serve in modest portions because it is very rich.

*To cleanse the palate . . .*

# CHAMPAGNE AND CRANBERRY COCKTAIL

Take a pitcher and pour 1 bottle of champagne or sparkling
wine gently down the side so as not to lose the fizz. Add 1 cup of
cranberry juice and a dash of angostura bitters and serve in a chilled
glass with a few fresh or frozen cranberries.

# BLUE CHEESE AND TURKEY SOUP

*Serves 6 to 8*

1½ quarts stock made from the turkey bones * 2 tbsp vegetable or olive
oil * 7 oz. celery * 3½ oz. carrots * 5 oz. onions * 5 oz. leeks * 5 oz.
potato * 1 tbsp plain flour * 8 oz. blue cheese * 1 cup cream

Coarsely chop all the vegetables. Heat the oil in a pan and cook the
vegetables over a low heat for 10 to 15 minutes until soft. Stir in the
flour, slowly add the stock, and let it all simmer for about 40 minutes.
Add the cream and blue cheese and stir until the cheese melts. Season

to taste. For a smoother finish, blend the soup in a food processor, but serve it as it comes if you want to keep it chunky and "rustic."

## MASHED POTATO WITH BLUE CHEESE AND TOASTED WALNUTS

5 oz. blue cheese ✳ 4 large potatoes ✳ 2½ oz. chopped walnuts ✳
¾ cup milk ✳ salt, pepper, and nutmeg

Make the mashed potato as normal, stirring in the milk and making sure there are no lumps. Toast the walnuts. Mix in the nuts, crumble in the blue cheese, and season to taste with salt, pepper, and nutmeg.

## TURKEY HASH

1 medium onion (chopped) ✳ 1 red pepper (deseeded and chopped)
✳ 2 waxy potatoes (chopped) ✳ olive oil ✳ 3 cups chopped turkey ✳
chopped sage (preferably fresh) ✳ 6 eggs ✳ 8 slices rindless bacon ✳
4 tbsp crème fraîche

Cook the onion, red pepper, and potatoes in ½ cup olive oil in a non-stick frying pan for about 10 minutes then set the veggies aside. Put the turkey and sage into a bowl with some salt and pepper. Beat the eggs and stir them into the turkey mix. Heat 2 tbsp oil in the pan and when hot pour in the turkey mixture so that it covers the pan and then the vegetables. Cook for about 5 minutes or until lightly browned, then turn and repeat on the other side. Start frying the bacon rashers at the same time as you start heating the oil. Serve by cutting into thick slices with a tablespoon of crème fraîche and crispy bacon rashers on the side.

# TURKEY CURRY

4 tbsp vegetable oil ✳ 1 medium onion (chopped) ✳ 4–5 garlic cloves
(finely chopped) ✳ 1 tbsp tomato purée ✳ 1 tsp ground cumin ✳ 1 tsp
ground coriander ✳ ½ tsp turmeric ✳ ¼ tsp cayenne powder ✳ ¼ tsp
garam masala ✳ 1-inch cube of ginger (chopped) ✳ ½ tsp salt ✳ 1 lb.
roast turkey (in chunks) ✳ 1 tbsp lemon

(If you don't have garam masala or turmeric, you can go on regardless.
If you don't have any of the spices, for example, if you are a student, use
curry powder instead.) Heat 3 tbsp oil in a saucepan and fry the onion
and garlic until the onion has softened and browned
on medium heat. At the same time, using a
small bowl or cup, mix the tomato purée
with a tablespoon of oil, the cumin,
coriander, turmeric, cayenne, garam
masala, ginger, and salt. When you
have a thick paste, stir it into the
onion mixture and fry for about
a minute. Stir in the turkey for a
minute and add 1¼ cups of hot
water and let it all simmer gently for
about 5 minutes. Add the lemon juice.
Garnish with coriander, if you have any,
and serve with basmati rice and a simple
green salad.

# HAM AND PEA RISOTTO

4 tbsp butter ✳ 3½ cups frozen peas ✳ 2 cups chopped ham ✳ 1
small onion, chopped ✳ 1½ quarts hot stock (perhaps from your
turkey) ✳ 2¼ cups risotto rice ✳ Parmesan

Melt the butter, stir in the chopped onion, and cook till softened. Add
the chopped ham and the peas and stir for 1–2 minutes. Add roughly
a quarter of the stock and the rice. Let it bubble for a few minutes and
then pour in the rest of the hot stock. Simmer gently. Be careful not
to stir it too much in case you break the peas. If it starts to dry out, add
some more stock or, if you've run out, some hot water. When the rice is
cooked, stir in some grated Parmesan.

# HOT HAM CAESAR SALAD

Assemble ¹/₂ lb. ham sliced into strips, I romaine lettuce torn into strips, I cup of croutons, shavings of Parmesan, a handful of parsley, 4 soft-boiled eggs cut into quarters, 2–3 anchovies per serving, and a dollop of mayonnaise. Toss the lettuce, croutons, Parmesan, and parsley in the mayonnaise. Flash-fry the slices of ham and lay them over the lettuce mix with the eggs and the anchovies.

## Salads

Below are some simple salad suggestions, using chopped or shredded turkey:

* *Toss the meat with toasted, unsalted cashews and/or broken walnuts, sliced fresh mango or oranges, and salad leaves.*

* *Cook thin rice noodles and let them cool. Stir in white turkey meat, some torn lettuce, chopped scallions, shredded carrot and/or cucumber, and dress with a mixture of soy sauce and sweet chili sauce.*

* *Cook some couscous and let it cool. Stir through chunks of turkey, diced red pepper, canned chickpeas (drained and rinsed), cubes of feta cheese, baby tomatoes chopped into halves or quarters, and a handful of pitted black olives.*

* *Boil or steam some green beans and let them cool. In a bowl, mix them with the turkey, some natural yogurt or mayonnaise, lemon juice, chopped red peppers and, if you want some tang, a handful or two of crumbled blue cheese.*

# THE VICAR

CHRISTMAS DAY 2006 STARTED FOR ME, AS EVER, WITH THE MIDNIGHT service, which is one of my favorite moments of the year. There's always a fantastic, buzzing atmosphere in the church at this service; an air of joy and anticipation. You can feel the accumulated magic of everyone's childhood memories of Christmas, secular and religious. When it is over and everyone has melted away into the dark, the glow and the thrill are quickly replaced by an eerie "after-the-party" feel in the echoing silence of the church.

This time, when I walked down through the churchyard and across the road to my home I was surprised to see the lights on. As I shut the door behind me, the kids were just heading upstairs to bed, but my wife, Edwina, was still hard at work in the kitchen. Our dog, Widget, had broken into the pantry and eaten all the vegetables she'd prepared and a number of other Christmas goodies. It wasn't until four in the morning that she finally climbed into bed after redoing everything.

I sat up in bed committing to memory the two sermons I was to give in the morning and it was about two thirty when I was happy that it was all safely logged and I could turn out the light.

When the alarm went off at six thirty, I was so tired I had to check I wasn't dead. When I staggered into the bathroom and saw my haggard face staring back at me in the mirror, my belief in the resurrection was strengthened still further! But that's Easter, isn't it? I washed and dressed and, after feeding the pigeons as I do every morning, I drove up to the little church of St. Nicholas in the middle of the village to conduct the eight o'clock Christmas Communion service. I was so sleepy it felt like I was having an out-of-body experience at first, but there was a great turnout and by the end it had become a really joyous service. On my way home for breakfast I dropped in at the local post office shop to greet Brian, who gets up earlier than any of us. The rectory was buzzing with activity when I got back. Edwina was shuffling various dishes of food between pantry, oven, and microwave, the rest of the family were rushing about in various states of undress, and Widget sat in the corner looking sheepish and ashamed. And quite right too.

On to St. Mary's, the bigger of the two churches in the parish, for the main ten o'clock service and body and soul were feeling more united now. Again, the church was packed to the rafters and, as at St. Nicholas's, the atmosphere was both worshipful and convivial. It felt as if I had shaken hands with half of the city by the time the last of the congregation had ambled away. I sat down by the crib for a few moments' peace before heading home, bathing in the wonder of this day when God rolled up his sleeves and entered the world of his own creation. I thought of the Christmas faces of my past, from childhood to the present day, who had all helped make what, for me, is the greatest day in the calendar.

We were just about to sit down at the table when a parishioner called in with the alarming news that a gravestone had been dug up and taken away. With my heart racing and a lump in my throat, I headed straight up to the churchyard. Sure enough, the stone of someone who had been buried only a few weeks earlier was indeed missing. It must have been vandals, I thought, but just to make sure before calling the police I rang the stonemason. "Blast it! I forgot to tell you," he said apologetically. "I took it away yesterday to work on over the Christmas break. I meant to call you!" Panic over.

The dinner was delayed but it was worth the wait because Edwina had done us proud. In spite of Widget's best efforts to ruin the day, it was a wonderful occasion as neighbors joined the family for the meal. After exchanging gifts, playing some games in the living room, and taking our guests home, I went up to bed at about ten thirty. I sat up for a while going over the events of the day in my head and, after kissing Edwina good night, a profound thought struck me. Widget had eaten everything he could find in the larder—except the Brussels sprouts. Even dogs hate Brussels sprouts! I smiled and rolled over. Wow, I love Christmas!

THE REV. CANON DAVID PARKER, parish of Lavant

# Bring in the Trees
## The Origins of Christmas Traditions

THE SOUND OF DISGRUNTLED PEOPLE BLEATING INTO THEIR BEARDS about the reduced role of Christianity in modern Christmas celebrations has been humming in the background for so long now that it has almost become a Christmas custom in its own right. Perhaps it is a tradition that we should preserve for future generations because, like all our other Christmas customs, it has virtually nothing to do with honoring the birth of Christ. It is a fact, as plain as the boil on the end of my nose, and one well worth passing on to the louder Christmas carpers in our midst, that every significant Christmas tradition we practice today, bar building a Nativity scene, has its origins not in Christian teaching, let alone the Bible, but in ancient pagan customs or nineteenth-century commercial initiatives. Bringing a Christmas tree into the home, kissing under the mistletoe, exchanging gifts, indulging in a large feast, throwing parties, lighting up the street with colorful illuminations, decorating the house with holly and ivy, lighting candles, burning the Yule log—these are all versions of customs practiced for centuries by our pre-Christian ancestors. (Sending Christmas cards and pulling crackers, meanwhile, have nothing to do with Christianity *or* paganism. They are the inventions of enterprising Victorians.) The truth is that the early Church authorities quickly realized that Christianity had a better chance of surviving and thriving if they incorporated into the Christian experience those wintertime pagan rituals which, for thousands of years, had formed a central part of so many European cultures. If they forced a break with the pre-Christian past, the Church risked alienating the very people they were so desperately trying to convert or to keep on board.

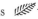

SOME CHURCHES CONTINUE TO **FORBID THE USE OF MISTLETOE** IN Christmas decorations. The early Christian Church in Britain was willing to ignore or even embrace other pagan customs, but it made great efforts to ban the use of mistletoe because of its strong associations with the powerful Druids. The Church suggested holly as an evergreen alternative, claiming that the plant's sharp leaves represented the thorns of Christ's crown on the cross and the berries were the drops of his blood. In Brittany mistletoe is known as *Herbe de la Croix* because it was believed that Christ's cross was made from the wood. According to the Breton legend, mistletoe was once a tree but was reduced to a parasite after the crucifixion.

❄ ❄ ❄ ❄

SCANDINAVIAN LORE HAS AN EXPLANATION FOR how mistletoe ended up at the top of trees. The legend goes that Frigga, wife of Odin and goddess of love and beauty, banished the mistletoe to the forest canopy after her son, Balder the Beautiful, was slain by a dart made from its wood. When Balder came back to life three days later, Frigga made mistletoe a symbol of **love and eternal life**.

❄ ❄ ❄ ❄

THE CUSTOM OF **KISSING UNDER THE MISTLETOE** HAS ITS ANCIENT origins in our ancestors' belief that the plant conferred powers of fertility and vitality. Some even considered it an aphrodisiac, owing to the allegedly sexual nature of the plant (Y-shaped branches, white sticky juice of ball-shaped berries—in fact, let's not go there). As recently as late medieval times, women were in the habit of wrapping mistletoe around their waists and wrists to increase their chances of conceiving. This belief arose partly from the fact that, like other evergreens, mistletoe's life force was so strong that it could live through the harshest of winters and even produce fruit. The mistletoe's way of reproducing and surviving without any roots in the ground led our ancestors to believe it had magical properties. On closer scientific inspection, however, there is little that might be considered "sexy" in the way the plant goes about the business of reproducing. In fact, it's about as erotic as a bucket of iced water down a naked back: mistletoe reproduces itself through bird shit. This is how it works: birds swallow plant's berries, birds crap on branch, seeds in droppings germinate in the bark, mistletoe grows, and excitable, unenlightened pagan ancestors jump up and down, grunting something unintelligible along the lines of "Wow, that plant's grown out of nothing!" Sometimes the process begins when the birds (often the mistle thrush) finish gorging themselves on the berries and find their beaks covered in sticky juice, which they proceed to wipe off on the bark of the tree. Mistletoe takes its name from this very process of reproduction, *mistel* being the Anglo-Saxon word for dung and *tan* the word for small branch.

❄ ❄ ❄ ❄

*It is hard to say exactly what is the origin of the English "kissing under the mistletoe," but the practice would appear to be due to an imagined relation between the love of the sexes and the spirit of fertility embodied in the sacred bough, and it may be a vestige of the licence often permitted at folk-festivals. According to one form of the English custom the young men plucked, each time they kissed a girl, a berry from the bough. When the berries were all picked, the privilege ceased.*

WASHINGTON IRVING
*The Sketch Book,* 1819–1820

❄ ❄ ❄ ❄

*The birthplace of the Christmas-Tree is Egypt, and its origin dates from a period long antecedent to the Christian era. The palm-tree is known to put forth a shoot every month and a spray of this tree with twelve shoots on it was used in Egypt at the time of the winter solstice as a symbol of the year completed. The palm-tree spray of Egypt, on reaching Italy, became a branch of any other tree (the tip of the fir was found most suitable from its pyramidal or conical shape) and was decorated with burning tapers lit in honour of Saturn, whose saturnalia were celebrated from the 17th to the 21st of December, the period of the winter solstice.*

*Illustrated London News,* December 1854

Evergreen trees have been used to celebrate pagan winter festivals for thousands of years. In northern Europe, the fir tree was the most common evergreen, and our ancestors used branches of fir to decorate their homes from the winter solstice through to spring. Evergreens were seen as symbols of eternal life at a time of year when all other forms of plant life had died off or gone into hibernation. The people of southern Europe—and beyond—also venerated evergreens during the winter months. The Romans used fir trees to decorate their temples during the rowdy December festival of Saturnalia. The Christians **commandeered the evergreen tradition**, and turned its symbolism of everlasting life to their own theological advantage.

\* \* \* \*

The first references in print to Christmas trees come from Germany in the early sixteenth century, but Riga, the capital of Latvia, likes to claim that its citizens erected the first tree in public in the year 1510. Not much is known about the erection of the Riga tree other than that men in black hats turned up, held a short ceremony of an indeterminate nature and then promptly burned the tree—which doesn't sound very Christmassy. My money's on the Germans.

\* \* \* \*

Indeed, all trails lead back to Germany when you try to hunt down the origins of the Christmas tree. As with so many Christmas customs, it is **impossible to say** exactly when, how, and why the fir tree came to be used as a central feature of Christmas decorations. But it is clear that there were stirrings in the snow-covered forests of the German territories, and the sound of axe upon bark, long before the rest of the Christian world had thought about bringing an entire tree into their home. The PR department of the Lutheran Church—or at least its sixteenth- or seventeenth-century equivalent—liked to claim that it was Martin Luther himself, the German founder of Protestantism, who first came up with the idea of having a decorated tree in the home. The story goes that Martin was stumbling through some wintry woods looking at the stars twinkling through the snow-dusted fir trees when, Eureka! the penny dropped. Why not chop one of these chaps down, he thought, and cover it with candles in honor of Christ's birth? Nice try, but I think not. There is not a scrap of historical documentation to back up this claim, so the most likely explanation is that the introduction of the Christmas tree was merely the logical extension of the pagan custom of bringing branches of evergreens into the home.

AS GERMAN EMIGRANTS HEADED TO THE UNITED STATES BY THE SHIPLOAD and German royals married into other European dynasties in the eighteenth and nineteenth centuries, they introduced many of the Christmas customs of their homeland to their adopted countries. A number of towns in the United States with German connections like to claim to have put up the country's first official Christmas tree, but what is certain is that the Christmas tree tradition came to the United States with the regiments of Hessian troops serving under British command during the American Revolution, as well as with German immigrants settling in Pennsylvania and Ohio. The first reference to a Christmas tree in the British Royal household comes in the reign of the Hanoverian George III and it was his German-born wife, Queen Charlotte, who is credited with its introduction at Windsor Castle in the late 1700s.

✼ ✼ ✼ ✼

IT WASN'T UNTIL AROUND 1850 that Christmas trees became a commonplace feature in British homes. Following his marriage in 1840 to Queen Victoria, the German nobleman Albert of Saxe-Coburg and Gotha was keen to import some German customs into the royal household, particularly at Christmas, which he regarded as a special time for the family. Victoria was only too happy to make him feel at home and before long Windsor Castle was **ablaze with giant fir trees**, dripping with gifts, confectionery, and dozens of carefully placed tapers. Today we take Christmas trees for granted but they must have been a spectacular and thrilling sight for the couple's young children. In 1848, an illustration of the royal family gathered around their decorated tree was published in the popular *Illustrated London News*. Within a few years every middle-class family worth its name would have a Christmas tree of their own.

✼ ✼ ✼ ✼

*It is that childish, open-hearted simplicity which, so it seems to me, makes Christmas essentially German, or at any rate explains why it is that nowhere else in the world does it find so pure an expression. The German is himself simple, warm-hearted, unpretentious, with something at the bottom of him which is childlike in the best sense. He is the last "Naturmensch" [child of nature] in civilization. Christmas suits him as well as a play suits an actor for whose character and temperament it has been especially written.*

MS. I. A. R. WYLIE
*My German Year*, 1910

HANDEL'S *MESSIAH* HAS LONG BEEN associated with Christmas but the famous oratorio was written as a piece for Easter. Handel, depressed and in debt at the time, was approached by his friend Charles Jenners to compose an oratorio based on Jenners's own recent arrangement of the Scriptures. Handel shelved his plans to return to his native Germany and, working from his home at 25 Brook Street in his adopted London, wrote the entire work in a remarkable **24-day burst** at the end of the summer of 1741. "I did think I did see all Heaven before me and the great God himself," Handel said of its composition. The *Messiah* was first performed in Dublin in April the following year.

❄   ❄   ❄   ❄

*A Christmas tree may be made at home for a very trifling cost. Long as they have been in fashion in England for juvenile parties, or for Christmas Eve, these trees seem to be still in favour almost as much as ever. Christmas trees may be covered with paltry trifles, or made the medium for dispensing suitable gifts amongst the members of the household.... The ordinary Christmas tree is covered with miscellaneous articles, some of more value than others, which are either distributed at hazard by the lady deputed to cut them down, or lots are drawn out of a bag of numbers corresponding to those fixed on the little presents themselves.*

Cassell's Book of the Household, 1878

## Top 5 most performed Christmas songs in the U.S.

1. The Christmas Song: Chestnuts Roasting on an Open Fire (written by Mel Tormé, Robert Wells; performed by Nat "King" Cole)
2. Have Yourself a Merry Little Christmas (written by Ralph Blane, Hugh Martin; performed by The Pretenders)
3. Winter Wonderland (written by Felix Bernard, Richard B. Smith; performed by Eurythmics)
4. Santa Claus Is Coming to Town (written by Fred Coots, Haven Gillespie; performed by Bruce Springsteen)
5. White Christmas (written by Irving Berlin; performed by Bing Crosby)

(Source: 2001–2005 survey for the American Society of<br/>Composers, Authors, and Publishers, published November 2006)

*When rosemary, and bays, the poet's crown,*
*Are bawl'd in frequent cries through all the town,*
*Then judge the festival of Christmas near,*
*Christmas, the joyous period of the year.*
*Now with bright holly all your temples strow,*
*With laurel green and sacred mistletoe.*
*Now, heav'n-born Charity, thy blessings shed;*
*Bid meagre Want uprear her sickly head:*
*Bid shiv'ring limbs be warm; let plenty's bowl*
*In humble roofs make glad the needy soul.*

JOHN GAY (1685–1732)
*Trivia, or the Art of Walking the Streets of London*

❄ ❄ ❄ ❄

"HUNTING THE WREN" IS ONE OF THE MORE UNFATHOMABLE CHRISTMAS customs practiced over the centuries by the British and Irish (and French to a lesser extent). Dozens of historians and folklore experts have failed to produce a satisfactory explanation of its meaning or origins. It has all but died out in England but it is still practiced in remote pockets of Ireland. Customs varied from country to country, district to district and century to century, but they were all versions of the same theme. During the Christmas period, the men of the village or town, sometimes in costume, would set out to kill a wren and fasten its body to the top of a long pole. They carried it in procession to all the houses, singing a special song and demanding money or a gift. In Ireland, one of the many variations of the song begins:

*The wren, the wren, the king of all birds,*
*On St. Stephen's Day was caught in the furze,*
*Although he is little, his family is great,*
*I pray you, good landlady, give us a treat.*

When every house had been visited, the procession headed to the churchyard where the wren was buried in a solemn ceremony. Historians suspect that the origins of this custom are as old as any in our culture, stretching back many centuries, even millennia, before the Christian era. The most plausible explanation goes like this: the little wren is known as "the king of birds," and for many centuries it was considered highly sacred. To kill one was regarded as the height of bad luck—except during the winter solstice, when it was customary for our primitive ancestors to slaughter a divine animal.

❊ ❊ ❊ ❊

*The time-honoured epoch for taking down Christmas decorations from Church and house is Candlemas Day, February 2nd. Terribly withered they are by that time. Candlemas in old times represented the end of the Christmas holidays, which, when "fine old leisure" reigned, were far longer than they are now. Every particle ought to be removed long before for cleanliness' sake, and not, as old Herrick puts it, because—*

*For how many leaves there be,*
*So many goblins you shall see*

*But when decorations were kept up till Candlemas in those merry old times, there was no gas, nor was the atmosphere of the house heated as it is today; there were too many chinks and crevices for that. It is found desirable now, in many houses, to remove them after Twelfth Day, January 6th (the Epiphany or Jour Des Rois); and by that time they are quite dusty and dirty enough, and everybody (except the children) is tired of holiday-making and ready to return to the sober business of life.*

*Cassell's Book of the Household, 1878*

❊ ❊ ❊ ❊

CHRISTMAS LIGHTS BEGAN TO APPEAR IN AMERICAN SHOP WINDOWS in about 1900 but it wasn't until after World War II that the majority of households could afford them.

❊ ❊ ❊ ❊

IN 1941, NOT LONG AFTER THE ATTACK ON PEARL HARBOR, UK Prime Minister Sir Winston Churchill stood side by side with Franklin Roosevelt outside the White House for the **annual lighting of the national tree**. There was no ceremony the following two years owing to wartime electricity restrictions. In 1963, Lyndon Johnson delayed the start of the ceremony until a 30-day period of mourning for the assassinated John F. Kennedy had passed. In 1979, Jimmy Carter canceled the ceremony in honor of the Americans being held hostage in Iran. The following year he ordered it lit for just 417 seconds—one for every day the hostages had been held.

*I have been looking on, this evening, at a merry company of children assembled round that pretty German toy, a Christmas Tree. The tree was planted in the middle of a great round table, and towered high above their heads. It was brilliantly lighted by a multitude of little tapers; and everywhere sparkled and glittered with bright objects. There were rosy-cheeked dolls, hiding behind the green leaves; and there were real watches (with movable hands, at least, and an endless capacity of being wound up) dangling from innumerable twigs; there were French-polished tables, chairs, bedsteads, wardrobes, eight-day clocks, and various other articles of domestic furniture (wonderfully made, in tin, at Wolverhampton), perched among the boughs, as if in preparation for some fairy housekeeping; there were jolly, broad-faced little men, much more agreeable in appearance than many real men—and no wonder, for their heads took off, and showed them to be full of sugar-plums; there were fiddles and drums; there were tambourines, books, work-boxes, paint-boxes, sweetmeat-boxes, peep-show boxes, and all kinds of boxes; there were trinkets for the elder girls, far brighter than any grown-up gold and jewels; there were baskets and pincushions in all devices; there were guns, swords, and banners; there were witches standing in enchanted rings of pasteboard, to tell fortunes; there were teetotums, humming-tops, needle-cases, pen-wipers, smelling-bottles, conversation-cards, bouquet-holders; real fruit, made artificially dazzling with*

gold leaf; imitation apples, pears, and walnuts, crammed with surprises; in short, as a pretty child, before me, delightedly whispered to another pretty child, her bosom friend, "There was everything, and more." This motley collection of odd objects, clustering on the tree like magic fruit, and flashing back the bright looks directed towards it from every side—some of the diamond-eyes admiring it were hardly on a level with the table, and a few were languishing in timid wonder on the bosoms of pretty mothers, aunts, and nurses—made a lively realisation of the fancies of childhood; and set me thinking how all the trees that grow and all the things that come into existence on the earth, have their wild adornments at that well-remembered time.

Being now at home again, and alone, the only person in the house awake, my thoughts are drawn back, by a fascination which I do not care to resist, to my own childhood. I begin to consider, what do we all remember best upon the branches of the Christmas Tree of our own young Christmas days, by which we climbed to real life. Straight, in the middle of the room, cramped in the freedom of its growth by no encircling walls or soon-reached ceiling, a shadowy tree arises; and, looking up into the dreamy brightness of its top—for I observe in this tree the singular property that it appears to grow downward towards the earth—I look into my youngest Christmas recollections!…

Among the later toys and fancies hanging there—as idle often and less pure—be the images once associated with the sweet old Waits, the softened music in the night, ever unalterable! Encircled by the social thoughts of Christmas-time, still let the benignant figure of my childhood stand unchanged! In every cheerful image and suggestion that the season brings, may the bright star that rested above the poor roof, be the star of all the Christian World! A moment's pause, O vanishing tree, of which the lower boughs are dark to me as yet, and let me look once more! I know there are blank spaces on thy branches, where eyes that I have loved have shone and smiled; from which they are departed. But, far above, I see the raiser of the dead girl, and the Widow's Son; and God is good! If Age be hiding for me in the unseen portion of thy downward growth, O may I, with a grey head, turn a child's heart to that figure yet, and a child's trustfulness and confidence!

Now, the tree is decorated with bright merriment, and song, and dance, and cheerfulness. And they are welcome. Innocent and welcome be they ever held, beneath the branches of the Christmas Tree, which cast no gloomy shadow! But, as it sinks into the ground, I hear a whisper going through the leaves. "This, in commemoration of the law of love and kindness, mercy and compassion. This, in remembrance of Me!"

CHARLES DICKENS
*A Christmas Tree*, 1850

As you settle down to write your 87th Christmas card, with the clock striking midnight and the repetitive strain injury starting to bite, you can cheer yourself up by cursing the name of Sir Henry Cole. (Damn your eyes, Cole! Damn your eyes, Cole!) Cole was one of those restless Victorian enthusiasts who didn't like to put his feet up at the end of a day until (a) he had invented something or (b) he had founded or constructed something or (c) he had reformed something. After an early career in the Public Records Office (which he reformed, of course), Cole became a very busy man indeed. In 1850, as an active member of the Royal Academy, he took on the role of principal organizer of the Great Exhibition, a year later he was appointed Prince Albert's chief adviser, and for the rest of the decade he oversaw the foundation of what is now the Victoria and Albert Museum. He was also the man responsible for the introduction of public lavatories in England. It's amazing he found the time to go to the bathroom. Earlier, in December 1842, when the onus of reinventing Western civilization began to mount on his broad shoulders, Cole became frustrated that there was no time left in his manic schedule to send letters offering festive greetings to all his friends … so he **invented the printed Christmas card**. The cards were designed and printed by someone else and he simply scribbled his signature at the bottom. Bingo! At a stroke he had freed up a few more days to found, reform, and invent things. Cole commissioned artist John Calcott Horsley to design a card for him, which featured a slightly drunk-looking family raising a toast around a table, surrounded by a border of more worthy images of people feeding the poor and clothing the naked and so on. Just over 1,000 were printed and those that Sir Henry did not need were sold for one shilling.

❄ ❄ ❄ ❄

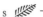 After the introduction of the "penny post" in 1840 and the modernization of the printing industry, the practice of **sending Christmas cards** began to catch on among the middle classes, but it wasn't until the 1860s that the cards were widely sold on the market. And it wasn't until the 1870s that the custom of sending one to every single person in the family address book, including the milkman, the mailman, and the funny-looking kid who delivers the logs, was firmly established.

❄ ❄ ❄ ❄

One strange Christmas custom that has fallen into disuse is the baking of the **Dumb Cake**. On Christmas Eve, a single girl wanting to discover her future husband prepared a cake, alone and in silence. She pricked the mixture with her initials and then left it in her bedroom before going to sleep with her door open. At midnight her husband-to-be was supposed to enter the room and leave his initials on the cake, and the girl would bake it the following morning. It's a wonder that custom ever died out.

✹  ✹  ✹  ✹

THE NEXT TIME YOU LIGHT A CHRISTMAS CANDLE, WRAP YOUR TREE IN lights, burn a Christmas log, or watch your local street illuminations being turned on, remember that you are continuing a winter tradition that stretches back to the very dawn of civilization. These **light and fire traditions** have become such an entrenched feature of Christmas that we have ceased to question why and how they have come to play such a central role. The answer, like so many, lies with our pagan ancestors and not with the teachings of the Church. During the winter solstice, fires were lit all over northern Europe to honor the rising of the sun and the lengthening of the days. People living off the fruit of the land worshipped the returning sun because it gave them the food they needed to live. At the same time as their northern cousins, the Romans also celebrated the winter solstice with the feast of Natalis Invicti Solis. In the east of the Roman Empire, the worship of the sun was equally widespread and formed the essence of the cult of Mithraism, which rivaled Christianity in the early days. The sun-god cult bore great resemblances to Christianity and was eventually absorbed by it.

---

### Christmas-related Cockney rhyming slang

| | |
|---|---|
| Mince pies—*Eyes* | Stand at ease—*Cheese* |
| Christmas Eve—*Believe* | Sugar candy—*Handy* |
| Christmas crackered— | Tom and Dick—*Sick* |
|    *Knackered* (tired) | Trashcan lids—*Kids* |
| Turtle doves—*Gloves* | Fine and dandy—*Brandy* |
| Box of toys—*Noise* | Left in the lurch—*Church* |
| Wobbly jelly—*Telly* (television) | Schindler's list—*Pissed* (drunk) |
| Plates and dishes—*Missus* (wife) | |

Cockney is the traditional name for working-class East Londoners, many of whom today still use a peculiar rhyming dialect to communicate with each other.

How **Boxing Day** came to acquire its name is a matter of minor dispute among historians and etymologists. From Victorian times until fairly recently, December 26 was the day on which better-off households gave gifts to servants, tradesmen, and the local poor, often presented in boxes. (The modern practice of giving Christmas bonuses to employees is thought to be an extension of this custom.) Another theory contends that the name dates back to the late Middle Ages when alms boxes were placed in churches for the collection of donations, which were handed to the poor on the day after Christmas. Boxing Day is an institution of the British Commonwealth and is not recognized or kept in the United States or elsewhere. In the UK, Australia, and Canada, it developed into a public holiday from the old tradition of giving servants the day off, in recognition of all the work they put in during the preparation of the Christmas Day celebrations. ("There we go, Miss Atkins, you have a nice lie-down today, and here's a box of candied carrots in gratitude for the 23-hour days you've been working for the past three months....")

❄ ❄ ❄ ❄

St. Stephen became the first Christian martyr after he was stoned to death by crowds in Jerusalem for speaking against the Temple and the Law. He is the **patron saint of horses** and his feast day falls on December 26, which explains Boxing Day's ancient association with horse activities. In Germany horses were once ridden around churches on St. Stephen's Day and in parts of England men bled them to encourage good health for the coming year. Today, hunts and race meetings continue the traditions.

THE TRADITION OF EATING **TWELFTH NIGHT Cake**, now virtually extinct, was for centuries a central feature of Christmas celebrations. The cook mixed various items into a rich fruitcake, each of which said something about the people who found them. If you found the dry bean, you were the king or queen; if you got the clove, you were a crook; if you got the twig you were a fool and if you were served the rag you were, er, a slag.

❄ ❄ ❄ ❄

THE TRADITION OF BUYING **POINSETTIAS** AS POTTED plants at Christmastime comes from Mexico, via the United States. Native to southern Mexico, Central America, and Africa, they are named after Joel Roberts Poinsett, the first American ambassador to Mexico, who started importing them to the States in the late 1820s. There are all sorts of Latin American Christian legends about how the plant has come to be associated so closely with Christmas. But these are all nonsense and you should politely look the other way or, if you must, leave the room when someone starts to spout off about Mexican infants weeping tears of blood under a roadside plant on December 25.... The plain truth is that poinsettias look good at Christmastime: they flower in the winter and happen to come in red and green, the traditional colors of Christmas.

❄ ❄ ❄ ❄

UNTIL RECENT YEARS, THREE GENERATIONS OF THE ECKE FAMILY (Paul Sr., Paul Jr., Paul III) of Encinitas, California, enjoyed a **near-monopoly** in the poinsettia market, because they were privy to a horticultural secret that left their competitors floundering to keep up. The Eckes developed a technique of grafting two varieties together to create fuller, leafier plants with more branches than the originals. The Eckes managed to keep their technique within the family business for almost 60 years until university researchers in the mid-1990s discovered it for themselves and went public with their findings.

CHRISTMAS TREES ARE **GETTING SHORTER**, ACCORDING TO RECENT research by the University of Cambridge. After spraying spruce trees with various compounds over a three-year period, researchers found that the plants treated with nitrogen were significantly shorter and wider and more densely branched than the others. Higher nitrogen levels, found in common agricultural treatments such as fertilizers and animal sewage, stimulate a hormone called cytokinin. The hormone causes buds to grow from the stem and become branches, so trees start to grow outwards as well as upwards, stunting their normal height.

❄ ❄ ❄ ❄

THE CHRISTMAS CRACKER WAS INVENTED IN THE 1840S BY A HIGHLY ambitious English baker called Tom Smith. When he was old enough to set up his own business, the enterprising Smith traveled to Paris in search of new confectionery ideas. "Bon-bons," sweets wrapped in twists of colored paper, were popular in the French capital at the time and Smith returned to England with a cunning plan: his own bon-bons would contain a love motto. After the novelty sweets went on sale in 1847, Smith continued to develop his idea, dumping the candy, adding small gimmicky toys, lengthening the wrapper and, after exhaustive experimentation, adding **little explosive strips** which popped when pulled. The crackers, originally called "cosaques," quickly gained in popularity and were used at all manner of special events and occasions, not just Christmas. Smith's son Walter is credited with the introduction of paper hats as well as the replacement of love messages with witty sayings.

THERE HAS BEEN AN AWFUL LOT of nonsense written about how the custom of the **Christmas stocking** originally came into being. The most irksome version, and one of the most frequently circulated, involves St. Nicholas, the fourth-century Turkish bishop, who later turned into Santa Claus. It goes like this: once upon a time, a kindly nobleman, distraught over the death of his wife, squandered his fortune, leaving his three daughters without dowries and facing a life of spinsterhood. Hearing of the girls' plight, St. Nick immediately mounted his white horse and rode like the wind to offer help. Keen to remain anonymous, for reasons unexplained, St. Nick hurtled by the nobleman's house and threw three pouches of gold coins into the air. Incredibly, all three of the pouches flew straight down the chimney and, even more incredibly, they somehow landed in three stockings that the three daughters just happened to have hung by the fireplace to dry. Sherlock Holmes, no doubt, would begin his investigation by asking: why three stockings, not six? Had the girls spent the day at a Turkish hopping competition in the local marsh? Call me cynical

if you wish, but you try running the "St. Nick stocking legend" past your seven-year-old child. You will be met with a face of stony incredulity. The most plausible explanation of the stocking seems to be that in various European countries, it was the custom to leave out some kind of receptacle (clog/sock/pouch) over the Christmas period, which was filled either by St. Nicholas, the patron saint of children (or some other Christian manifestation), or by some variation on the theme of a Christmas or winter spirit (fairy/troll/gnome/nice witch). In the early nineteenth century, the stocking beat off its rivals to become the preferred present receptacle of young children. This may have had something to do with the fact that a stocking can hold more gifts than a sock, and that the Dutch fashion of wearing uncomfortable wooden shoes never really caught on elsewhere. It's more likely, however, that Clement Clark Moore's reference to stockings in his famous poem "'Twas the Night Before Christmas" and Thomas Nast's subsequent illustrations of the poem simply popularized a custom that, up until then, was little known and practiced by only a few.

# THE RACEHORSE TRAINER

EVERY DAY IS A WORKING DAY FOR ME—ALL 365 OF THEM—AND Christmas Day is just like any other. The horses need feeding and exercising and the stables need mucking out. Horses never give you the day off. Also, Boxing Day is traditionally one of the big racing days of the year, and if we have any runners, they need to be given a good go on the gallops the day before. I realized last year (2006) that I have worked every Christmas Day for half a century. The needs of horses have changed little over the years, and virtually nothing in the way we look after them has changed since my father first started training racehorses back in 1955. We feed them, they shit, we clear it out, we give them fresh bedding, and take them out for a gallop.

I began by helping out my dad as a five-year-old, mucking out the stables and preparing the horse feed. I'd open the presents in my stocking from Father Christmas and then, at first light, my brother John and I would get dressed and head down the road to the stables with Dad. At the end of the morning, we'd get cleaned up and dressed for Christmas lunch with the family, and then, with a bellyful of turkey, it was back down to the stables to tend to the horses in the afternoon. Young horses need their exercise, so it's a nightmare if it has snowed or there's been a hard frost because we can't take them out into the fields for a gallop. We have a small exercise circle about 20 feet in diameter, but you can only do one horse at a time and they can't go round it faster than a trot.

Fortunately it doesn't snow much in the south of England these days, but I remember the incredible winter of 1962–1963 when a snowstorm blew in on Boxing Day, and the temperature dropped sharply. It didn't thaw out for three months. The lanes around the village were often filled with drifts as high as the hedges. I remember one of the horses getting stuck in a drift after leaping a fence and sinking up to her head in snow. Dad had a hell of a job dragging her out. As a young boy, that winter was a fantastic time. We missed a lot of school and spent day after day sledding on the South Downs and having snowball fights. Dad wasn't so happy about it, though, because it meant that the horses didn't get their exercise. He kept hoping the big thaw would come, but it wasn't until April that the ground was finally free. Almost all the race meetings across the country were canceled, from Boxing Day pretty well until the Cheltenham Festival in early spring.

I vividly remember going down to the stables with Dad as a young boy on Christmas Day, but since I was a teenager it's just a blur, one day being no different from any other. There is one Christmas Day, however, that I will never forget. It was in the mid-1980s and I was down at the stables finishing off my work for the morning when I heard a bit of a commotion on the road outside. I went out to see what was going on, and was met by the slightly alarming sight of about 50 cows careering through the narrow lane that leads into the heart of the village. Someone had left a gate open and the herd had just wandered out of the field and headed up along the road, past the pub and the stables and through the village, crashing into front gardens, trampling and munching them to destruction.

I immediately called the farmer and then went to see if I could help him herd them into somewhere safe until he decided what to do. In hindsight, I wish I'd gone home instead! The pressure of the rest of the herd had forced some of the cows into the big slurry pit halfway up the lane, and one of them had gone in so deep she had got stuck and was starting to get distressed. There was no way she was going to get out on her own, so I went back to the village and called the Fire Brigade. Somehow we had to get a belt around the cow so they could drag her out with the winch.

I'm still not too sure why it was me who ended up wading into that giant pool of muck and not the farmer or one of the firemen. I think the farmer had a bad back or something, and the firemen said they weren't used to dealing with cattle! That left Muggins. It was a proper nightmare. By the time I got to the cow and started to strap the belt around her I was up to my armpits in runny shit. The smell was horrendous. Gagging all the time, I finally managed to get the belt on and the firemen were able slowly to drag the cow clear. I walked the half-mile or so home, looking like a swamp monster. The turkey had just been taken from the oven when I walked into the house. "Merry Christmas!" I said to my wife, Sally. She just looked at me and said: "Maybe you should get changed before we sit down for lunch."

STEVE WOODMAN, racehorse trainer

# Turkey in the Trenches

## Christmas at War

ACCORDING TO THE MEDIEVAL code of chivalry, all warring factions were obliged to down their weapons over the Christmas period. By 1460, this honorable tradition appears to have fallen into disuse as Lancastrians and Yorkists butchered one other in the Battle of Wakefield on December 30. It was during this especially bloody battle of the Wars of the Roses, a victory for the Lancastrians, that Richard Duke of York and his son, the twelve-year-old Earl of Rutland, were killed and their bodies violated by the savage

"HELLO, SANTA!"
*Sgt. Will Neil, 10th Black Watch.*

Lord Clifford in acts so hideous that they swung public sympathy toward the Yorkist claim to the throne. After the Duke was killed, Clifford cut off his head, put a paper crown on top, and then stuck it on a pole and exhibited it on the city walls of York. Later, he caught up with the fugitive Earl of Rutland, and stabbed the prepubescent boy in the heart as he begged for mercy. His head found its way onto a pole alongside his father's.

❄ ❄ ❄ ❄

AS THE LUFTWAFFE INTENSIFIED its bombing blitz on London and other British cities in late 1940, *Good Housekeeping* magazine showed a flash of humor by suggesting readers make their Christmas cakes in the shape of an **Anderson air-raid shelter**.

❄ ❄ ❄ ❄

*Xmas Day. I must give an account of how we spent Xmas in camp. A good many of us received parcels from home containing cakes and puddings etc. These were heroically put on one side, until Xmas Day, then each man*

who had anything took a chum who had not received anything and shared with him, so that every man had a little taste of the homeland. On Xmas Eve there was a heavy fall of snow and Xmas morning we awoke to a fine morning and three or four inches on the ground. Then the fun started. The English and French formed sides against the Russians and then commenced a right battle royal. First the English rushed the Russian lines, with a terrible shout, the same shout doing more to dishearten the enemy than the actual snowballs. Charging and counter-charging was the order all the morning. For myself I have started to hold a series of Church of England services in a large empty tent. I was fortunate enough to get around 100 hymn books through the American Ambassador Mr. Gerrard at Berlin and these series of services are a great boon to the camp.

PTE. THOMAS RAINBIRD
Letter home from Doberitz prisoner-of-war camp, January 1915

❋ ❋ ❋ ❋

Winston Churchill had left Egypt on 11 December 1943 to fly home after the historic conferences with Allied war leaders at Cairo and Teheran. From that moment there had been a complete clamp-down on any news of his whereabouts.

He left Cairo intending to meet General Eisenhower at Tunis but his aircraft encountered an extraordinary series of blunders. The Prime Minister had left Cairo suffering from extreme exhaustion and by the following morning he was desperately ill with pneumonia.

When he rose from his bed ten days later, his mind was fully occupied with the Allied landing at Anzio. The naval Commander-in-Chief, Mediterranean, was bombarded with demands for information on the availability of Landing Craft for that invasion. As the Flag Lieutenant, I was instructed to accompany Admiral Sir John Cunningham to see the Prime Minister.

When we arrived at Mr. Churchill's headquarters we were joined by the top brass of the Mediterranean theatre headed by General Eisenhower, General Bedell-Smith, General Sir Henry Maitland-Wilson and Air Marshal Sir Arthur Tedder.

Mrs. Churchill was there with daughter Sarah, her son Randolph and the Prime Minister's physician, Lord Moran. I also recognized Mr. Churchill's watchdog, Detective Inspector Thomson, and met "Tommy" Thompson, Churchill's "personal assistant," and Desmond Morton, his "special investigator."

As the most junior officer present, I decided to move into the only unoccupied corner before anyone asked me searching questions. Then Mr. Churchill entered the room, shook my hand, and inquired, "How are you on this glorious Christmas morning? I have asked you and several other young officers here today because I thought you might have a more said. "It was touch and go. When he was in a critical state he said to me, 'Thompson, if this is the end it is well that I should die in sight of Carthage.'"

At dinner Mr. Churchill dined in his bedroom with his senior guests but afterwards he returned to talk to the rest. His entry into the room produced a remarkable effect with everyone, including the most eminent Generals and Air Marshals, assuming an air of rigid and deferential alertness, and stammering halting replies to any questions he asked. It took me back to my schooldays. At any moment any of us from Eisenhower, the head of the school, to Pawle, the most junior new boy, might be confronted with some shocking neglect of duty by the new headmaster.

"The Knave of Spades"

agreeable Christmas with me than you would in your Algerian fastness." He then left the room and a surprising number of complete strangers gathered around me, convinced that Mr. Churchill had imparted some information of great importance, and I saw no reason to disillusion them.

When lunch time arrived we were sharply deflated. While the rest of the guests filed into the dining room we were banished to a spartan guesthouse and a meal of granite-hard bacon and worm-riddled vegetables, served on a dirty tin plate and accompanied by a mug of lukewarm coffee. Just as we finished this unappetizing meal a messenger arrived to tell us that there had been a mistake and that a lavish lunch of turkey and Christmas pudding was waiting for us.

We listened spellbound to Mr. Churchill who was at the top of his form. I asked the detective if the rumours of the P.M.'s illness had been exaggerated. "Not at all," he

But on that Christmas night so many years ago Winston Churchill seemed only concerned that for all his guests and particularly the younger officers, this should be an occasion they would recall all their lives.

I was to see Mr. Churchill many times again. I was even to write a book about him with the great man's blessing. But that first Christmas meeting on the shores of the Bay of Tunis, when he returned from the shadows to take a leading part in the making of history, was the most memorable of all.

GERALD PAWLE,
"Christmas with Churchill"
*Blackwoods Magazine*, December 1973

NEWSPAPERS THROUGHOUT THE ALLIED WORLD REPORTED CHURCHILL'S **pneumonia** with varying degrees of alarm, but by the final week before Christmas it seemed as if the worst had passed and the *News of the World* was able to run the headline "Premier's Pneumonia Subsiding." The irregularity of the premier's pulse appeared to be the cause of the greatest anxiety and the paper quoted a doctor as saying, "This seems to indicate that the illness has thrown some strain on his heart. This could be partly accounted for by recent pressure of work lowering the patient's resistance at his age.... Mr. Churchill must still be regarded as seriously ill."

❄ ❄ ❄ ❄

KURT ZEHMISCH WAS A GERMAN SCHOOLTEACHER WHO FOUGHT IN THE trenches on the Western Front in the 134th Saxon Regiment. His war diaries were discovered in an attic near Leipzig in 1999. Below he describes the friendly exchanges that took place between the Germans and British over Christmas 1914. On Christmas Eve the shooting stopped and a few soldiers from each side emerged from the trenches, shook hands in no-man's-land, and agreed not to shoot the following day:

*Afterwards, we placed even more candles than before on our kilometre-long trench, as well as Christmas trees. It was the purest illumination—the British expressed their joy through whistles and clapping. Like most people, I spent the whole night awake. It was a wonderful, if somewhat cold night.... The English brought a soccer ball from the trenches, and pretty soon a lively game ensued. How marvellously wonderful, yet how strange it was. The English officers felt the same way about it. Thus Christmas, the celebration of Love, managed to bring mortal enemies together as friends for a time.*

The British troops who fraternized with Zehmisch and his comrades were the men of the Royal Welch Fusiliers, the battalion of Robert Graves and Siegfried Sassoon. In his book *The War the Infantry Knew*,

Captain J. Dunn, a medic in the Royal Welch, recorded how hostilities resumed on Boxing Day:

*At 8:30 I fired three shots in the air and put up a flag with "Merry Christmas" on it, and I climbed on the parapet. He put up a sheet with "Thank you" on it, and the German Captain appeared on the parapet. We both bowed and saluted and got down into our respective trenches, and he fired two shots in the air, and the war was on again.*

*The first Canadian troops of World War II began to arrive in Britain in the week before Christmas in 1939. They docked in Liverpool after crossing the Atlantic in five cruise liners with the officers billeting in suites and the men in first-class cabins. The division of 7,400 men was assembled in less than three months, which was hailed as a great feat considering the country had a standing army of just 4,500 men, 5 mortars, and 16 tanks.*

❋ ❋ ❋ ❋

THERE WAS NO RATIONING IN Britain during Christmas 1939, the first year of World War II. Public morale was still high and everyone spent freely in the shops—partly because rationing was planned to start early in the New Year and people were determined to **enjoy themselves while they could**. The most popular gifts that year, not surprisingly, carried a military theme or a practical purpose. Boys received figures of servicemen in uniforms, and toy aircraft and tanks, while dolls of Red Cross nurses were a popular choice for girls. Many grown-ups gave each other steel helmets and fancy gas-mask cases. The following year it was clear that the economic hardships of war had started to bite: the most popular gift was soap.

❋ ❋ ❋ ❋

*"Peace Upon Earth!" was said. We sing it,*
*And pay a million priests to bring it.*
*After two thousand years of mass*
*We've got as far as poison gas.*

THOMAS HARDY (1840–1928), "Christmas, 1924"

THE TURNING POINT OF THE AMERI-
can War of Independence came on
Christmas night 1776 when General
George Washington, the future first
president of the country, led what
remained of his small demoralized
army of patriots across the icy waters
of the Delaware River. Just after dawn
on Boxing Day, the American army
of 2,400 soldiers **stormed the New
Jersey town of Trenton**, quickly
overwhelming the 1,500 German
mercenary troops fighting for the
British. (The Trenton troops, many
of them still in bed, were said to
be nursing hangovers from their
Christmas Day celebrations.) As a
military engagement, the battle was a
non-event, but the date is regarded as

GEORGE·WASHINGToN

hugely significant in the destiny of the North American continent.
The surprise attack brought the Americans their first victory
in the war and boosted flagging morale across the anti-British
communities of the colony after a series of major defeats, mainly in
the New York area. One of the small handful of patriots seriously
wounded in the skirmishes was an eighteen-year-old lieutenant
called James Monroe, who in 1817 would become the fifth president
of the United States. Monroe was hit in the shoulder by a musket
ball and had lost great quantities of blood before a doctor clamped a
severed artery, saving his life by a matter of minutes.

❄ ❄ ❄ ❄

*Christmas Day No Firing. An unofficial armistice
took place and troops of both sides met and buried
the dead. The Battalion fixed up a board with
"A merry xmas" written on it in German midway
between the trenches and was evidently much
appreciated by the enemy.*

2ND WILTSHIRE WAR DIARY, Friday, December 25, 1914, France

So we stumbled along our now hard, frosted ditch, and scrambling up on to the bank above, strode across the field to our next bit of trench on the right. Every one was listening. An improvised Boche band was playing a precarious version of "Deutschland, Deutschland, über Alles," at the conclusion of which, some of our mouth-organ experts retaliated with snatches of ragtime songs and imitations of the German tune. Suddenly we heard a confused shouting from the other side. We all stopped to listen. The shout came again. A voice in the darkness shouted in English, with a strong German accent, "Come over here!" A ripple of mirth swept along our trench, followed by a rude outburst of mouth organs and laughter. Presently, in a lull, one of our sergeants repeated the request, "Come over here!"

"You come half-way — I come half-way," floated out of the darkness.

"Come on, then!" shouted the sergeant. "I'm coming along the hedge!"

… After much suspicious shouting and jocular derision from both sides, our sergeant went along the hedge which ran at right-angles to the two lines of trenches. He was quickly out of sight; but, as we all listened in breathless silence, we soon heard a spasmodic conversation taking place out there in the darkness.

Presently, the sergeant returned. He had with him a few German cigars and cigarettes which he had exchanged for a couple of Machonochie's [canned stew] and a can of Capstan [tobacco], which he had taken with him. The séance was over, but it had given just the requisite touch to our Christmas Eve, something a little human and out of the ordinary routine.

After months of vindictive sniping and shelling, this little episode came as an invigorating tonic, and a welcome relief to the daily monotony of antagonism. It did not lessen our ardour or determination; but just put a little human punctuation mark in our lives of cold and humid hate. Just on the right day, on Christmas Eve! But, as a curious episode, this was nothing in comparison to our experience on the following day.

On Christmas morning I awoke very early and emerged from my dug-out into the trench. It was a perfect day. A beautiful, cloudless blue sky. The ground hard and white, fading off towards the wood in a thin low-lying mist.

*"Fancy all this hate, war, and discomfort on a day like this!" I thought to myself. The whole spirit of Christmas seemed to be there, so much so that I remember thinking, "This indescribable something in the air, this Peace and Goodwill feeling, surely will have some effect on the situation here to-day!" And I wasn't far wrong …*

*… Walking about the trench a little later, discussing the curious affair of the night before, we suddenly became aware of the fact we were seeing a lot of evidences of Germans. Heads were bobbing about and showing over the parapet in a most reckless way, and, as we looked, this phenomenon became more and more pronounced.*

*A complete Boche figure suddenly appeared on the parapet, and looked about itself. This complaint became infectious. It didn't take "Our Bert" [the British sergeant who exchanged goods with the Germans the previous day] long to be up on the skyline. This was the signal for more Boche anatomy to be disclosed, and this was replied to by our men, until in less time than it takes to tell, half a dozen or so of each of the belligerents were outside their trenches and were advancing towards each other in no-man's land.*

*I clambered up and over our parapet, and moved out across the field to look. Clad in a muddy suit of khaki and wearing a sheepskin coat and Balaclava helmet, I joined the throng about half-way across to the German trenches.*

*… Here they were—the actual practical soldiers of the German army. There was not an atom of hate on either side that day; and yet, on our side, not for a moment was the will to beat them relaxed. It was just like the interval between the rounds in a friendly boxing match. The difference in type between our men and theirs was very marked. There was no contrasting the spirit of the two parties. Our men, in their scratch costumes of dirty, muddy khaki, with their various assorted head-dresses of woollen helmets, mufflers and battered hats, were a light-hearted, open, humorous collection as opposed to the sombre demeanour and stolid appearance of the Huns in their grey-green faded uniforms, top boots, and pork-pie hats.*

*These devils, I could see, all wanted to be friendly; but none of them possessed the open, frank geniality of our men.*

CAPTAIN BRUCE BAIRNSFATHER, ROYAL WARWICKSHIRE REGIMENT
from his book *Bullets and Billets,* 1916

Bairnsfather, who returned to England in 1915 after he was injured, became the best-known cartoonist of the Great War. He was sent back to the Front in the role of "Officer Cartoonist" and his amusing illustrations were widely credited with helping to keep up the morale of the Commonwealth troops.

*No better Christmas dinner was eaten that day in the whole United States. Invincible youth was around the board, and the two colonels lent dignity to the gathering, without detracting from its good cheer.*

*The table had been set late, and soon the winter twilight was approaching. As they took another slice of ham they heard the boom of a cannon on the far side of the Rappahannock. Harry went to the window and saw the white smoke rising from a point about three miles away.*

*"They can't be firing on us, can they, sir?" he said to Colonel Talbot. "They wouldn't do it on a day like this."*

*"No. There are two reasons. We're so far apart that it would be a waste of good powder and steel, and they would not violate Christmas in that manner. We and the Yankees have become too good friends for such outrageous conduct. If I may risk a surmise, I think it is merely a Christmas greeting."*

*"I think so, too, sir. Listen, there goes a cannon on our side."*

*… Then they listened, as the echo of the twelfth Southern shot died away on the stream, and no sound came after it. Twenty-four shots had been fired, twelve by each army, conveying Christmas good wishes, and the group in the house went back to their dinner. Some glasses had been found, and there was a thimbleful of wine, enough for everyone. The black cake was cut, and at a word from Colonel Talbot all rose and drank a toast to the mothers and wives and sweethearts and sisters they had left behind them.*

*Then the twilight thickened rapidly and the winter night came down upon them, hiding the ruined town, the blackened walls, the muddy streets and the icicles hanging from scorched timbers.*

JOSEPH A. ALTSHELER
*The Star of Gettysburg,* 1915

*Our regiment spent Christmas in camp and on duty. We thought of home and knew that many a stocking would not be found in its accustomed place, and the usual Christmas dinners and parties likely in many homes would be omitted because of fathers and sons in the army. I recall our cooks made extra efforts to have something nice for dinner on this Christmas day. We had pork and beans that had been roasted and baked all night in a bed of hot coals for dinner, boiled rice with good sale molasses or muscavade sugar, old government Java coffee, nice hard tack (worms all shook out), sweet potatoes, and corned beef, and all this cooked in good shape. We thought it a dinner fit for a king and all were merry.*

RALPH STURTEVANT, 13th Infantry, December 25, 1862,
on Christmas Day in Virginia during American Civil War

✳ ✳ ✳ ✳

"**I wish**
th.t every one of you could spend Christmas in Blighty." As that isn't possible I'll wish again—— that good friends at home will remember this Christmas to send out plenty of Waterman's Ideals. You deserve to have the Best.

*Christmas Day. Work done on parapets. "C" Coy in firing line and "A" relieved "D" Coy. Enemy very quiet as a whole. C.Q.M.S. Merritt was instantaneously killed whilst unloading rations from the trolley head by a Whiz bang [artillery shell].*

6TH WILTSHIRE WAR DIARY,
Saturday, December 25, 1915, France

*I send you, my sailors and soldiers, hearty good wishes for Christmas and the New Year. My grateful thoughts are ever with you for victories gained, for hardships endured, and for your unfailing cheeriness. Another Christmas has come around, and we are still at war, but the Empire, confident in you, remains determined to win. May God bless you and protect you. At this Christmastide the Queen and I are thinking more than ever of the sick and wounded among my sailors and soldiers. From our hearts we wish them strength to bear their sufferings, speedy restoration to health, a peaceful Christmas and many happy years to come.*

KING GEORGE V, Christmas message to his troops, 1916

❋ ❋ ❋ ❋

WOMAN'S WEEKLY, THE POPULAR MAGAZINE, CAME UP WITH A raft of practical and inexpensive homemade gift and decoration suggestions for Christmas in December 1939. Gift ideas included *a dainty organdie [stiff muslin] lampshade … a necklace of flowers … an embroidered linen stamp book cover … a dressing table container for powdering pads … a crinoline lady tea cosy [knitted] … quickly knitted heelless bed socks …* An advertisement by retailers Henry Jones offered readers a series of *gay little purses* in the form of military headwear.

*This is not a fireside chat on war. It is a talk on national security; because the nub of the whole purpose of your President is to keep you now; and your children later, and your grandchildren much later, out of a last-ditch war for the preservation of American independence and all of the things that American independence means to you and to me and to ours.... Never before since Jamestown and Plymouth Rock has our American civilization been in such danger as now.... The Nazi masters of Germany have made it clear that they intend not only to dominate all life and thought in their own country but also to enslave the whole of Europe, and then to use the resources of Europe to dominate the rest of the world.... Some of our people like to believe that wars in Europe and in Asia are of no concern to us. But it is a matter of most vital concern to us that European and Asiatic war- makers should not gain control of the oceans which lead to this hemisphere. It is no exaggeration to say that all of us in the Americas would be living at the point of a gun—a gun loaded with explosive bullets, economic as well as military.... Frankly and definitely there is danger ahead—danger against which we must prepare. But we well know that we cannot escape danger, or the fear of it, by crawling into bed and pulling the covers over our heads.... If Great Britain goes down, the Axis powers will control the continents of Europe, Asia, Africa, Australasia, and the high seas—and they will be in a position to bring enormous military and naval resources against this hemisphere.... The people of Europe who are defending themselves do not ask us to do their fighting. They ask us for the implements of war, the planes, the tanks, the guns, the freighters, which will enable them to fight for their liberty and our security. Emphatically we must get these weapons to them in sufficient volume and quickly enough, so that we and our children will be saved the agony and suffering of war which others have had to endure. Let not defeatists tell us that it is too late. It will never be earlier. Tomorrow will be later than today.... American industrial genius, unmatched throughout the world in the solution of production problems, has been called upon to bring its resources and talents into action. Manufacturers of watches, of farm implements, linotypes, cash registers, automobiles, sewing machines, lawn mowers, and locomotives are now making fuses, bomb-packing crates, telescope mounts, shells, pistols, and tanks.... We must be the great arsenal of democracy. For us this is an emergency as serious as war itself. We must apply ourselves to our task with the same resolution, the same sense of urgency, the same spirit of patriotism and sacrifice, as we would show were we at war.... As President of the United States I call for that national effort. I call for it in the name of this Nation which we love and honor and which we are privileged and proud to serve. I call upon our people with absolute confidence that our common cause will greatly succeed.*

PRESIDENT FRANKLIN D. ROOSEVELT's famous Christmas holiday
radio address to the American people, 1940

*Dear Eq, I have received your letter & Christmas card for which many thanks. You seem to be having a toffee time for a soldier, what with your Christmas cards & your straw mattresses & 3 blankets—3 blankets! Think of your old pal sleeping on a waterproof sheet laid on cold wet clay, with all his clothes and overcoat on—both of which are sodden with clay—and covered with a soaking wet blanket. It's an absolute fact that when we come out of the trenches I, with the help of another, wrung the water out of my blanket and overcoat, when dry stood up by itself! Still while I may envy you, I do not grudge you your comfort. Be as comfortable as you can while you can.... We were in the trenches again for three days before and on Christmas Day and were relieved on Boxing morning.... We had decided to give the Germans a Christmas present of 3 carols and 5 rounds rapid. Accordingly as soon as night fell we started & the strains of "While Shepherds" (beautifully rendered by the choir) arose upon the air. We finished that and paused preparatory to giving the 2nd item on the programme. But lo! We heard answering strains arising from their lines. Also they started shouting across to us. Therefore we stopped any hostile operations and commenced to shout back. One of them shouted, "A Merry Christmas English. We're not shooting tonight." We yelled back a similar message & from that time until we were relieved on Boxing morning @ 4am not a shot was fired. After this shouting had gone on for some time they stuck up a light. Not to be outdone, so did we. Then up went another. So we shoved up another. Soon the two lines looked like an illuminated fete.... Next morning, Christmas Day, they started getting out of the trenches & waving & some came towards us. We went out and met them & had the curious pleasure of chatting with the men who had been doing their best to kill us, and we them. I exchanged a cigarette for a cigar with one of them (Not a bad exchange eh?) & as some of them spoke English had quite a long conversation. One fellow said that as soon as the war was over he was "going back to England by express." He had a wife and 2 children in the Alexander Rd!!*

PTE. ERNEST MORLEY, 1/16th Londons, diary entry,
December 29, 1914, "Somewhere in France"

❄ ❄ ❄ ❄

CHRISTMAS 1941 WAS AN ANXIOUS TIME FOR THE PEOPLE OF THE United States following the devastating Japanese attack on the Pacific fleet at anchor in Pearl Harbor on December 7, in which 2,403 people were killed. The following day Congress took just 20 minutes to vote for a declaration of war. There wasn't even a debate. The declaration read, *"The President is hereby authorized and directed to employ the entire naval and military forces of the United States and the resources of the Government to carry on war against the imperial Government of Japan; and, to bring the conflict to a successful termination, all of the resources of the country are hereby pledged by the Congress of the United States."* The response of the American people to the call for arms was impressive as the country shelved its plans for a peaceful Christmas and prepared for conflict. Hundreds of thousands of young men volunteered or were drafted into the services, swelling the ranks of the U.S. Army alone from 174,000 in September 1939 to 5.4 million by the end of 1942.

GNEISENAU
SCHARNHORST

ON BOXING DAY 1943, BRITAIN INFLICTED A SIGNIFICANT BLOW ON the German fleet when Royal Navy ships sank the German battle cruiser *Scharnhorst* in the Arctic. Together with its equally formidable sister ship the *Gneisenau* (they were known to the British as the "ugly sisters"), the *Scharnhorst* had caused major disruption to the convoys bringing vital supplies to Britain and Russia from the United States. Enigma, the British code-breaking machine, decoded German naval signals, revealing that the *Scharnhorst*, which had recently sunk the British cruiser *Rawalpindi*, was on its way to attack an Anglo-American convoy to Russia. In what became known as the Battle of the North Cape, the 31,000-ton battle cruiser was surprised by the British battleship *Duke of York* and a number of cruisers. After a day-long chase and battle, the giant *Scharnhorst* sank to the ocean's floor with the loss of almost 2,000 men. Only 36 survived. That night Admiral Bruce Fraser on board the *Duke of York* urged his officers: "Gentlemen, the battle against *Scharnhorst* has ended in victory for us. I hope that if any of you are ever called upon to lead a ship into action against an opponent many times superior, you will command your ship as gallantly as *Scharnhorst* was commanded today."

*Sandy:* "LEND ME A FRANC, TAM."
*Tam:* "NA, I CANNA DAE THAT."
*Sandy:* "IT'S A SMA' THING TO REFUSE."
*Tam:* "AY, BUT YOU WOULDNAE PAY ME BACK, AND THEN YOU AN' ME WAD QUARREL; SO WE MAY JUST AS WEEL QUARREL NOO, WHILE THE MONEY'S IN MY POCKET."

*Horace Gaffron.*

*I think I have seen one of the most extraordinary sights today that anyone has ever seen. About 10 o'clock this morning I was peeping over the parapet when I saw a German, waving his arms, and presently two of them got out of their trenches and some came towards ours. We were just going to fire on them when we saw they had no rifles so one of our men went out to meet them and in about two minutes the ground between the two lines of trenches was swarming with men and officers of both sides, shaking hands and wishing each other a happy Christmas.*

2ND LIEUTENANT DOUGAN CHATER, 2nd Gordon Highlanders, in a letter to his
mother from a trench near Armentières, Christmas Day 1914

*Christmas has a special meaning for American soldiers in Vietnam. Amid the tragedy and ugliness of war, the Holy Season reminds us of the joy and beauty of peace. In a land whose people struggle for a better life, the Christmas message brings cheer and hope for the future. You who serve in this distant land may be justly proud. The spirit of Christmas is expressed each day in your actions toward our gallant allies and in your sacrifices for our country's cause. My warmest wishes to you and to your families on this Christmas Day.*

MESSAGE FROM W. C. WESTMORELAND, General, U.S. Army Commanding, written on Christmas Day menus for U.S. troops on active duty in Vietnam

❄ ❄ ❄ ❄

*We had a white Xmas here and it began to snow on Xmas eve, and we had about six weeks of it. It kept on freezing day and night all the time, and were snowed up and frozen up then, but we had our happy Xmas Day on New Years Day after coming out.*

*Our Christmas dinner in the line or shell holes was composed of tins of bully beef and a few hard biscuits thrown into a canteen, with a big handful of snow to make water. We could make some Bully Stew for dinner that day and we enjoyed it fine, as there was nothing else to have at that time. Snow the only thing to make water as we couldn't use the water in our bottles we carried for it. It was a crime then which would have won us 14 days pay stopped, and we didn't want that now.*

*The ground was covered in snow and the water in the shell holes was frozen. We were not supposed to use it or drink it at any time. We had to be very careful about lighting a fire because of the smoke in the daytime and the light of the fire at night as well. If Jerry had seen it we may have had a gentle visitor come over to visit us and wish us a Happy Xmas and a Xmas box to wish us a happy New Year all in one day....*

*We had our real Christmas dinner on New Years day better late than never. We had a whole pig for a company of men, and also Xmas pudding which came up to us in tins, and so much beer for each man and cigs and a good concert at night. Some of the men got drunk and drowned their joys and sorrows in beer and some sang them away. It was blinking cold for us. A few days later Jerry came over and dropped a few hard boiled eggs, or bombs close by our camp, on some transport lines and laid out a number of men for us, just to wish us all a happy new year.*

PTE. ALFRED LEWIS, 6th Northamptons, 1917

*The nation has made a resolve that war or no war, the children of England will not be cheated out of the one day they look forward to all year. So, as far as possible, this will be an old-fashioned Christmas, at least for the children.*

MINISTRY OF INFORMATION FILM
*Christmas under Fire*, 1941

❄ ❄ ❄ ❄

*Christmas and New Year's were very pleasantly remembered in this winter camp, though observed somewhat differently than they had been on former occasions and in other places. Still the American will ever remember his holidays, and, if possible, celebrate them with such ceremonies as his ingenuity may suggest or his means and condition enable him to improve. We had "select" dinner parties, with rare entertainment; music by our excellent band, speeches, and minor festivities of a more general character. One of the incidents of Christmas day was a procession formed by all who were permitted to be festive, headed by a donkey, the gravest ass of the company, mounted by an impersonation of Old Nicholas. This procession moved about the camp to the music of fife and drum, much to the amusement of both the participants and the lookers-on. Lieutenant-Colonel Chandler nominally commanded this merry expedition, but the donkey, being a little obstinate and difficult to ride in a straight line, really became the solemn chief of the occasion. There were other far more brilliant exhibitions with and around us, but probably none where the participants became more innocently jolly.*

CHAPLAIN EDWIN MORTIMER HAYNES,
*A History of the 10th Vermont Regiment*, 1870

❄ ❄ ❄ ❄

AT THE START OF THE SECOND BOER WAR IN 1899, BEFORE SIGNIFICANT reinforcements had arrived in the Cape, the British suffered a number of military setbacks that horrified the public back home. In the week before Christmas, known as "Black Week," the British suffered heavy casualties and the towns of Mafeking and Ladysmith were besieged by marauding Boer forces who swarmed over the

borders from their traditional homelands.
The situation was so grave that Queen
Victoria, now in her 81st year, broke with
tradition and remained at Windsor Castle
to host a Christmas Day tea for the wives
and families of soldiers serving in southern
Africa. The following day she wrote in her
diary:

*All the women and children trooped in, and after looking at the tree they all sat
down to tea at two very long tables, below the tree. Everyone helped to serve
them, including my family, old and young, and my ladies and gentlemen.*

*I was rolled up and down round the tables, after which I went away for a
short while to have my own tea, returning when the tree was beginning to be
stripped, handing myself many of the things to the wives and dear little children…
there were some babies of a few weeks and months old…. It was a very touching
sight, when one thinks of the poor husbands and fathers, who are all away, and
some of whom may not return. They seemed all very much pleased.*

❄ ❄ ❄ ❄

IN THEIR CHRISTMAS-WEEK ISSUE OF 1939, *WOMAN'S WEEKLY*
encouraged housewives to cheer up their anti-shatter blackout
blinds, insisting:

*There is no reason why the precaution of pasting strips of paper on our windows should
make them look so depressingly ugly. With a little ingenuity they can be extremely
attractive for Christmas time…. Use black paper cut into three-quarter inch strips
which, when posted diagonally, will give the effect of leaded diamond panes. Then
find a pretty wall paper border, cut it out, and paste it all around the edge of the
window…. You will be surprised what a difference this makes to your room.*

❄ ❄ ❄ ❄

*Of course you're doing some entertaining this Christmas, not just for your family
and lifelong friends, but for some of our new friends from across the Atlantic. I
know you won't let food restrictions deter you from offering hospitality you will
all enjoy so much. After all, it seems only right that some of the lease-and-lend\**
*foods should be used for this purpose. What shall we give the American boys to
make them feel at home? Try some typical American dishes. You're going to like
them so much that they are certain to become part of English menus from now on.*

*If tea is the meal you can best manage, it would be hard to beat … Apple Sauce
Cake … Peanut Cookies, Spiced Pork and Cabbage and Baking Powder Biscuits.*

*Woman's Pictorial* magazine, **December 19, 1942**

\* Supplies to Europe from America under lease-and-lend agreement.

It was Christmas '44 and we were obviously looking round for a Christmas dinner. Although turkeys in that part of Italy at that time were very plentiful, it seemed to be that every place we got to and wanted a turkey, the Canadians had got there first. And they had more or less cleared the place of turkeys for their Christmas. So we thought "I don't know, we're going to be without a Christmas dinner" and somebody suggested that one or two nights before we'd come through a farm, a big farm, where there were a lot of pigs. We decided to go back to this farm and see what we could get. This was at night-time. We took the truck back to this farm and we came away with a little pig. The only way we could get this pig away …—and this may sound terrible—the only way to stop it grunting was to stick your fingers up its nostrils so it couldn't make a noise. And somebody knew how to do this apparently—and this was done. So we got it in the back of the truck and going back we had to go back through a road patrol, which was manned by MPs [Military Police]. So of course we were very undecided how we were going to get the pig through the patrol. So we covered the pig over in the back of the truck, hence the two fingers up his nostrils to keep him quiet, and somehow or other we got through the patrol. The thing was—where to keep the pig? Where we were billeted were like flats with verandas and we got this pig up into one of the flats and we just blocked it in and let it loose on the veranda. Well, that was all right until the CO came out in the morning and looked up and saw the pig running around. He wants to know who's responsible and of course we owned up. I said I was one of them.

He [the CO] was what we used to call "one of the boys"—although he was a Major he was a very nice fellow—and I said "Well look, it's obvious we're *going to be stuck here for Christmas and the lads of course had no Christmas dinner. So we decided to go out and get some." So his words were: "You can't keep the bloody thing up there forever, so you've got to find somewhere for it to go ..." Anyway, to cut a long story short—on the day before Christmas we had to approach the cook staff to kill the pig and cook it. So this was agreed upon, providing the Officers' Mess had a leg—so we agreed to this—we had to. So of course the pig was killed and roast and cooked and a happy ending to a Christmas—except for the pig!*

JOHN ALBERT LUXFORD, NCO,
1st Bn King's Royal Rifle Corps (IWM archives)

❋ ❋ ❋ ❋

THE FINAL CHRISTMAS OF WORLD WAR II WAS PROBABLY THE MOST difficult. The British were worn down by six years of conflict, bereavement, and increasing deprivation, and their hopes that the war would be over by the end of 1944 were dashed by events on the front. Three dozen V1 and V2 Doodlebug missiles struck towns and cities in northern England, reminding people that though Germany was on the retreat, technology still allowed her to strike deep into enemy territory. Many cities had almost completely run out of alcohol, which only compounded the sense of gloom. There was some good news, though, with the relaxation of blackout laws, which allowed people to **illuminate their homes** for the first time since the war began. The Ministry of Food also increased rations of sweets, sugar, and meat, but the general hardship is reflected in the issuing of instructions on how people might decorate their homes ... with vegetables.

# THE SERVICEMAN

I WAS A FEW MONTHS INTO MY FIRST TOUR OF NORTHERN IRELAND, which perhaps explains why I was chosen to work the Christmas Day shift, alongside "Mongo," another Navy pilot, in one of the squadron's Sea Kings. From late evening through to the small hours of Boxing Day, we were scheduled to carry out a whole variety of tasks across South Armagh: moving troops, supporting the police, and transporting supplies and equipment between the many army bases and outposts strung out across "bandit country." It was just another routine mission in Ulster, but flying at night and at low-level is as demanding and challenging as helicopter flying gets, even without terrorists taking pot shots at you.

We were based at Aldergrove airbase next to Belfast International airport, and it was from there that Mongo and I prepared to set off in the afternoon of Christmas Day. The rest of the lads were teasing us as they settled down in the Runway Club, the makeshift officers' mess where we used to congregate for a few beers. We couldn't go out much in Belfast, for obvious security reasons, so most of our entertaining and drinking was done in that little prefab hut. When some of us had gone into the city center for a night out a few weeks earlier, it had almost ended in disaster. We were happily chatting to some local girls when one of the boys let slip that he had spent the day working in "bandit country." The girls immediately twigged who we were, put down their drinks and turned on their stiletto heels. They walked straight over to a group of heavy-looking lads at the bar and started pointing at us. All military personnel in Northern Ireland are under the strictest orders not to get into trouble with the locals and so, abandoning our pints where they stood, we took off as fast as we could. We all scattered in different directions before making our separate ways back to our car. When we got there we realized that Midge—a young guy also on his first tour of the province—was missing. We were beginning to fear the worst when we heard a muffled noise coming from the trunk. It was Midge. He thought it the safest place to wait until the rest of us arrived!

As the lads put on their paper hats and settled down to their turkey dinner, Mongo and I put on our helmets and night-vision goggles (NVGs) and lifted off into the rapidly fading light. It was pitch dark by the time we came in to land at the heavily fortified military base at Bessbrook, a huge old cotton mill in a staunchly republican area from where we supplied other military outposts. Going by road was not an option in the heart of bandit country. Everything was done by helicopter. It's a forbidding place, Bessbrook Mill, a bit like a high-security prison with its miles of barbed wire strung over the towering red-brick walls and corrugated-iron roofs. When we arrived and relieved the RAF crew, there was a boisterous atmosphere inside as the other soldiers and aviators were tucking into their Christmas dinners and generally getting into the festive spirit.

Mongo and I, the only aircrew working in South Armagh that evening, were getting a bit fed up with all this partying. You don't get many opportunities to let your hair down out in Ulster and we wanted a bit of the fun too, so our plan was to carry out our tasks as quick as possible and get back to Bessbrook a bit earlier than scheduled. But my heart sank when we went to pick up the timetable from Buzzard, the air transport coordinator, and realized that there was masses to do—thanks to our chums in the RAF, who had obviously dawdled on their shift and left us a backlog of tasks to clear. "RAF bastards!" we muttered in unison. As we headed out to the helicopter to start our shift, all the other pilots blew out their streamers at us and gave us a rude rendition of "Rudolph the Red-Nosed Reindeer."

We tried to execute our tasks as promptly and efficiently as possible, without taking any risks. Dozens of troops needed inserting and picking up from various locations across the county; we picked up a suspect arrested by the RUC; another RUC officer needed to be flown back to base for medical attention after slashing his leg open while pursuing a suspect. Flying at night is tiring at the best of times because you really have to concentrate with the NVGs on, especially when you are so low to the ground. It was perhaps fitting then that to cap a hard, crappy night's work we finished the shift by transporting a two-ton tub of soldier shit from one of the watchtowers back to base from where it could be taken away to be treated. It was five in the morning and the Christmas party was long finished by the time we finally crawled into our sleeping bags, exhausted and pissed off. "Well, happy bloody Christmas, bud!" I said to Mongo as I turned off the light by my bunk. There was a pause and then, out of the darkness, came the sound of a rather flat Christmas streamer being blown.

LT.-CDR. JONJO JOHNSON, Fleet Air Arm

# Happy Reunions, Terrible Tantrums

## Christmas and the Family

*Christmas came and except for the ceremonial Mass, the solemn and wearisome Christmas congratulations from neighbours and servants, and the new dresses everyone put on, there were no special festivities, though the calm frost of twenty degrees Reaumur, the dazzling sunshine by day, and the starlight of the winter nights seemed to call for some special celebration of the season.*

LEO TOLSTOY, *War and Peace*

*Christmas time! That man must be a misanthrope indeed, in whose breast something like a jovial feeling is not roused—in whose mind some pleasant associations are not awakened—by the recurrence of Christmas. There are people who will tell you that Christmas is not to them what it used to be; that each succeeding Christmas has found some cherished hope, or happy prospect, of the year before, dimmed or passed away; that the present only serves to remind them of reduced circumstances and straitened incomes—of the feasts they once bestowed on hollow friends, and of the cold looks that meet them*

now, in adversity and misfortune. Never heed such dismal reminiscences. There are few men who have lived long enough in the world, who cannot call up such thoughts any day in the year. Then do not select the merriest of the three hundred and sixty-five for your doleful recollections, but draw your chair nearer the blazing fire—fill the glass and send round the song—and if your room be smaller than it was a dozen years ago, or if your glass be filled with reeking punch, instead of sparkling wine, put a good face on the matter, and empty it off-hand, and fill another, and troll off the old ditty you used to sing, and thank God it's no worse. Look on the merry faces of your children (if you have any) as they sit round the fire. One little seat may be empty; one slight form that gladdened the father's heart, and roused the mother's pride to look upon, may not be there. Dwell not upon the past; think not that one short year ago, the fair child now resolving into dust, sat before you, with the bloom of health upon its cheek, and the gaiety of infancy in its joyous eye. Reflect upon your present blessings—of which every man has many—not on your past misfortunes, of which all men have some. Fill your glass again, with a merry face and contented heart. Our life on it, but your Christmas shall be merry, and your new year a happy one!

Who can be insensible to the outpourings of good feeling, and the honest interchange of affectionate attachment, which abound at this season of the year? A Christmas family-party! We know nothing in nature more delightful! There seems a magic in the very name of Christmas. Petty jealousies and discords are forgotten; social feelings are awakened, in bosoms to which they have long been strangers; father and son, or brother and sister, who have met and passed with averted gaze, or a look of cold recognition, for months before, proffer and return the cordial embrace, and bury their past animosities in their present happiness. Kindly hearts that have yearned towards each other, but have been withheld by false notions of pride and self-dignity, are again reunited, and all is kindness and benevolence! Would that Christmas lasted the whole year through (as it ought), and that the prejudices and passions which deform our better nature, were never called into action among those to whom they should ever be strangers!

The Christmas family-party that we mean, is not a mere assemblage of relations, got up at a week or two's notice, originating this year, having no family precedent in the last, and not likely to be repeated in the next. No. It is an annual gathering of all the accessible members of the family, young or old, rich or poor; and all the children look forward to it, for two months beforehand, in a fever of anticipation....

CHARLES DICKENS

*Sketches by Boz*: "A Christmas Dinner"

## 10 Christmastime survival tips

1. Get together and write a list of what everyone wants to do. Decide what is really important, and if possible prioritize.

2. Make a list of who needs to see who. Particularly important with extended stepfamilies.

3. Use a calendar. Make a note of which family members are doing what and when.

4. Schedule in some time to recharge your own batteries. If you're well rested you'll be able to enjoy your family more.

5. Don't try to do everything yourself. Make a list of jobs which need to be done and allocate them among the whole family.

6. Don't try to keep everyone happy all the time. You'll collapse under the pressure.

7. If this is your first Christmas as a stepfamily, your child may feel confused and maybe even angry. Try to allocate some time that you can spend alone together, to reassure them that your love for them has not changed.

8. Adults don't have to enjoy being with children all the time. Allow some time for you to be alone with your partner, other family members, or friends.

9. Don't assume that everyone else is having a wonderful time. Everyone else is muddling through just like you, so try not to put pressure on yourself.

10. Don't act in anger. If everything gets to be too much, remove yourself from the situation and perhaps call a friend or relative.

*The Little Strangs say the "good words" as they call them, before going to bed, aloud and at their father's knee, or rather in the pit of his stomach. One of them was lately heard to say "Forgive us our Christmases, as we forgive them that Christmas against us."*

SAMUEL BUTLER, English writer, c. 1890

*I was nine or ten years old when my father was sacked on Christmas Day. He was a manager, the results had not been good, he lost a game on December 22nd or 23rd. On Christmas Day, the telephone rang and he was sacked in the middle of our lunch.*

JOSÉ MOURINHO, soccer manager

❄ ❄ ❄ ❄

THERE ARE CHRISTMAS QUARRELS, AND THERE ARE CHRISTMAS quarrels. On December 25, 1929, North Carolina tobacco farmer Charlie Lawson, a hitherto respected local figure, went into a **murderous frenzy**, slaying his wife and six of their seven children before taking his own life. The murders inspired poems and songs, the most famous being "The Ballad of Charlie Lawson." The motives behind the mass murder remain a mystery, but police are refusing to rule out the possibility that Mr. Lawson may have lost at Scrabble.

❄ ❄ ❄ ❄

*After three days, guests and fish stink.*

JEWISH SAYING

ESTONIANS HAVE BEEN BEMUSED IN RECENT
years by the strange Christmas spectacle
of people—mostly ex-pat Englishmen and
Australians—playing cricket on a frozen lake in
Tallinn, the capital of the Baltic state.

❄ ❄ ❄ ❄

*December 24—I am a poor man, but I would gladly give ten
shillings to find out who sent me the insulting Christmas card I
received this morning. I never insult people; why should they
insult me? The worst part of the transaction is, that I find
myself suspecting all my friends....*

*Christmas Day—We caught the 10:20 train at
Paddington, and spent a pleasant day at Carrie's mother's.
The country was quite nice and pleasant, although the roads
were sloppy. We dined in the middle of the day, just ten of us, and
talked over old times. If everybody had a nice, uninterfering mother-in-law,
such as I have, what a deal of happiness there would be in the world. Being all in
good spirits, I proposed her health, and I made, I think, a very good speech.*

*I concluded, rather neatly, by saying: "On an occasion like this—whether
relatives, friends, or acquaintances—we are all inspired with good feelings
towards each other. We are of one mind, and think only of love and friendship.
Those who have quarrelled with absent friends should kiss and make it up. Those
who happily have not fallen out, can kiss all the same."*

*I saw the tears in the eyes of both Carrie and her mother, and must say I felt
very flattered by the compliment. That dear old Reverend John Panzy Smith,
who married us, made a most cheerful and amusing speech, and said he should
act on my suggestion respecting the kissing. He then walked round the table and
kissed all the ladies, including Carrie. Of course one did not object to this; but I
was more than staggered when a young fellow named Moss, who was a stranger
to me, and who had scarcely spoken a word through dinner, jumped up suddenly
with a sprig of mistletoe, and exclaimed: "Hulloh! I don't see why I shouldn't
be in on this scene." Before one could realise what he was about to do, he kissed
Carrie and the rest of the ladies.*

*Fortunately the matter was treated as a joke, and we all laughed; but it was
a dangerous experiment, and I felt very uneasy for a moment as to the result. I
subsequently referred to the matter to Carrie, but she said: "Oh, he's not much
more than a boy." I said that he had a very large moustache for a boy. Carrie
replied: "I didn't say he was not a nice boy."*

GEORGE AND WEEDON GROSSMITH
*The Diary of a Nobody,* 1892

IN THE 1840S ILLUSTRATIONS OF THE ROYAL family gathered around a heavily decorated Christmas tree appeared in the popular newspaper the *Illustrated London News*. In the years following, it became *de rigueur* for well-to-do households up and down the land to have a tree of their own in the home. It is difficult to overstate the moral and cultural influence the royal family held over the British public in Victoria's reign. "If it was good enough for Victoria and Albert, then it'll certainly do for us" was the prevailing attitude of the ever-expanding middle classes. Victoria's example, combined with the popularity of Dickens's Christmas tales, entrenched the notion of Christmas as a happy family event in people's minds.

❄ ❄ ❄ ❄

*Dear Dolly:*

*I wish you a merry Christmas, and want you to buy whatever you think you would like with the enclosed check for twenty dollars. It is now just forty years since you stopped being my nurse, when I was a little boy of seven, just one year younger than Quentin now is.*

*I wish you could see the children play here in the White House grounds. For the last three days there has been snow, and Archie and Quentin and their cousin, cunning little Sheffield Cowles, and their other cousin, Mr. John Elliott's little girl, Helena, who is a perfect little dear, have been having all kinds of romps in the snow—coasting, having snowball fights, and doing everything—in the grounds back of the White House. This coming Saturday afternoon I have agreed to have a great play of hide-and-go-seek in the White House itself, not only with these children but with their various small friends.*

THEODORE ROOSEVELT (1858–1919)
Letter to his old nurse Mrs. Dora Watkins
from the White House, December 19, 1905

*It was in this winter that his attention was particularly drawn to the festival of Christmas, which, apparently, he had scarcely noticed in London. On the subject of all feasts of the Church he held views of an almost grotesque peculiarity. He looked upon each of them as nugatory and worthless, but the keeping of Christmas appeared to him by far the most hateful, and nothing less than an act of idolatry. "The very word is Popish," he used to exclaim, "Christ's Mass!" pursing up his lips with the gesture of one who tastes asafoetida by accident. Then he would adduce the antiquity of the so-called feast, adapted from horrible heathen rites, and itself a soiled relic of the abominable Yule-Tide. He would denounce the horrors of Christmas until it almost made me blush to look at a holly-berry. On Christmas Day of this year 1857 our villa saw a very unusual sight. My father had given strictest charge that no difference whatever was to be made in our meals on that day; the dinner was to be neither more copious than usual nor less so. He was obeyed, but the servants, secretly rebellious, made a small plum-pudding for themselves. (I discovered afterwards, with pain, that Miss Marks received a slice of it in her boudoir.) Early in the afternoon, the maids—of whom we were now advanced to keeping two—kindly remarked that "the poor dear child ought to have a bit, anyhow," and wheedled me into the kitchen, where I ate a slice of plum-pudding. Shortly I began to feel that pain inside which in my frail state was inevitable, and my conscience smote me violently. At length I could bear my spiritual anguish no longer, and bursting into the study I called out: "Oh! Papa, Papa, I have eaten of flesh offered to idols!" It took some time, between my sobs, to explain what had happened. Then my father sternly said: "Where is the accursed thing?" I explained that as much as was left of it was still on the kitchen table. He took me by the hand, and ran with me into the midst of the startled servants, seized what remained of the pudding, and with the plate in one hand and me still tight in the other, ran until we reached the dust-heap, when he flung the idolatrous confectionery on to the middle of the ashes, and then raked it deep down into the mass. The suddenness, the violence, the velocity of this extraordinary act made an impression on my memory which nothing will ever efface.*

EDMUND GOSSE (1849–1928), English writer

*Father and Son*

❄ ❄ ❄ ❄

TWELFTH NIGHT WAS AN IMPORTANT EVENT FOR QUEEN VICTORIA and her family as the royal household brought the Christmas celebrations to a joyful, if mildly alarming, conclusion. Each year, a short play was staged by her children and a special Twelfth Night Cake was served. The family also settled down to a musical recital of some sort; very often it was a piece by Felix Mendelssohn, her favorite contemporary composer. **Parlor games** were a feature of the day too and the family favorite was an entertainment by which they all tried to grab raisins from a bowl of flaming brandy. The last person to go threw salt into the bowl to produce a bright yellow flame. Strip those Victorians of their whalebone corsets and waxed moustaches for the day, and golly, they knew how to party.

❄ ❄ ❄ ❄

*Christmas Day 1946: Drove to Midnight Mass at Nympsfield very slowly on frozen roads with Teresa, Bron [Auberon] and Vera [nursery maid] in the back of the car. The little church was so painfully crowded. We sat behind a dozen insubordinate little boys who coughed and stole and wrangled. The chairs were packed so tight it was impossible to kneel straight. Drove home very slowly and did not get to bed until 2:30 a.m.... I made a fair show of geniality throughout the day though the spectacle*

*of a litter of shoddy toys and half-eaten sweets sickened me. Everything is so badly made nowadays that none of the children's presents seemed to work. Luncheon was cold and poorly cooked. A ghastly day.*

EVELYN WAUGH (1903–66),
English writer
*Diaries*

*For Boxing Day, Grandma Osborne had perfected a pumpkin trick which turned all the cold Christmas pudding and mince pies suddenly into funeral baked meats. She did it almost on the stroke of five and in one wand-like incantation. Lying back in the Hymnal position, she would close her eyes, smile her thin gruel of a smile and say, "Ah well, there's another Christmas over." I dreaded the supreme satisfaction with which she laid the body of Christmas to rest. In one phrase she crushed the festive flower and the jubilant heart.*

JOHN OSBORNE (1929–1994), English playwright, *A Better Class of Person*

❄ ❄ ❄ ❄

*Each Christmas, at this time, my beloved father broadcast a message to his people in all parts of the world.... As he used to do, I am speaking to you from my own home, where I am spending Christmas with my family.... My father and my grandfather before him, worked hard all their lives to unite our peoples ever more closely, and to maintain its ideals which were so near to their hearts. I shall strive to carry on their work.*

EXTRACT FROM QUEEN ELIZABETH II'S FIRST CHRISTMAS MESSAGE, 1952

*We had a delightful Christmas yesterday—just such a Christmas thirty or forty years ago we used to have under Father's and Mother's supervision in 20th Street and 57th Street. At seven all the children came in to open the big, bulgy stockings in our bed; Kermit's terrier, Allan, a most friendly little dog, adding to the children's delight by occupying the middle of the bed. From Alice to Quentin, each child was absorbed in his or her stocking, and Edith certainly managed to get the most wonderful stocking toys. Bob was in looking on, and Aunt Emily, of*

course. Then, after breakfast, we all formed up and went into the library, where bigger toys were on separate tables for the children. I wonder whether there ever can come in life a thrill of greater exaltation and rapture than that which comes to one between the ages of say six and fourteen, when the library door is thrown open and you walk in to see all the gifts, like a materialized fairy land, arrayed on your special table?

U.S. PRESIDENT THEODORE ROOSEVELT,
letter to his sister, Mrs. Douglas Robinson, December 26, 1903

❋ ❋ ❋ ❋

*Every year on Christmas day I like to tell my mother that I'm a lesbian, even though I'm not. It just gets everything going.*

JENNY ECLAIR (1960– ), comedian

---

### 10 great **Christmas films for grown-ups**

It's a Wonderful Life
A Christmas Carol
Miracle on 34th Street
Trading Places
White Christmas
The Bishop's Wife

Christmas in Connecticut
Scrooged
National Lampoon's
    Christmas Vacation
Christmas with the Kranks

---

### 10 great **Christmas films for kids**

The Snowman
A Christmas Story
How the Grinch Stole
    Christmas
Gremlins
A Charlie Brown Christmas
A Christmas Carol

The Muppet Christmas
    Carol
Prancer
Rudolph the Red-Nosed
    Reindeer (1964 TV
    version)
Home Alone

*One of the least pleasing effects of modern refinement is the havoc it has made among the hearty old holiday customs. It has completely taken off the sharp touchings and spirited reliefs of these embellishments of life, and has worn down society into a more smooth and polished, but certainly a less characteristic surface. Many of the games and ceremonials of Christmas have entirely disappeared, and, like the*

*sherris sack of old Falstaff, are become matters of speculation and dispute among commentators. They flourished in times full of spirit and lustihood, when men enjoyed life roughly, but heartily and vigorously; times wild and picturesque,*

*which have furnished poetry with its richest materials, and the drama with its most attractive variety of characters and manners. The world has become more worldly. There is more of dissipation, and less of enjoyment. Pleasure has expanded into a broader, but a shallower stream; and has forsaken many of those deep and quiet channels where it flowed sweetly through the calm bosom of domestic life. Society has acquired a more enlightened and elegant tone; but it has lost many of its strong local peculiarities, its homebred feelings, its honest fireside delights. The traditional customs of golden-hearted antiquity, its feudal hospitalities, and lordly wassailings, have passed away with the baronial castles and stately manor-houses in which they were celebrated. They comported with the shadowy hall, the great oaken gallery, and the tapestried parlor, but are unfitted to the light showy saloons and gay drawing-rooms of the modern villa.*

WASHINGTON IRVING

"Christmas" from *The Sketchbook, 1831*

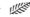

1. Avoid unrealistic expectations and rigid plans
2. Exercise
3. Resist the temptation to self-medicate with too much alcohol
4. Don't feel pressured to be the life and soul of the party
5. Negotiate plans to avoid conflict
6. Try to find some time for yourself.

CHRISTMAS IS MORE STRESSFUL than divorce or burglary for millions of people, according to research carried out in 2006. One in twenty of those questioned said they would prefer their marriage to break down or their house to be broken into rather than play host to family and friends over the holiday period. Entertaining guests and enforced good humor are the main causes of stress. The Samaritans say they receive a huge jump in calls from people worried by debt or depressed by loneliness over the Christmas period. The charity offers six key tips for reducing Christmas stress:

ONE MINUTE YOU'RE BLITHELY pulling down your pants and sitting on the photocopier at the office party after downing a six-pack, and the next you're shuffling down the Family Planning aisle in the drugstore wearing dark glasses and a false beard with the strange guy from Accounting. According to the people who keep a close watch on these things, the expression "family Christmas" in recent times has come to assume an entirely different meaning for many young people. Apparently more people have **unprotected sex** during the festive period than at any other time of the year.

# THE DISC JOCKEY

I'VE WORKED ON CHRISTMAS DAY FOR MOST OF MY ADULT LIFE AND it's only recently, since I had my children, that I've been at home for the entire day. Working at Christmas never used to bother me when I was younger. In fact, I jumped at the chance of getting away from the tension that tends to build up at home as the day goes on and the relatives pour in the door. Christmas was the high season for arguments in our house!

With a job in television or radio, you soon get accustomed to working unsociable hours. Over the years, I grew used to slipping into the house in the small hours of Boxing Day morning, and quietly making myself a cold turkey sandwich before slipping up to my bedroom. Inevitably, the countertops would be covered in all the washed-up plates and dishes and I'd feel quietly pleased that, once again, I had managed to escape the Christmas mayhem and the marathon post-meal clean-up.

The one time I didn't feel like working on Christmas Day was in 1986, the year I got married. Missing Christmas is no great sacrifice when you're single, but that year I really wanted to be snuggled up with my husband. I was working as a vision mixer for GMTV in those days and there was no chance of getting the day off. That particular Christmas Day was also memorable because the producers took the slightly risky decision to squeeze every single person in the building into the final shot of the program. The entire production crew plus the cleaners, security guards, the guy in the coffee shop round the corner—anyone who happened to be in the vicinity—all dropped what they were doing, and came on to the set and surrounded Anne Diamond and Nick Owen on the sofas. Once the crowd had assembled, the cameramen set their cameras to wide angle, locked them off, and ran round to join us. It was a fantastically chaotic scene as everyone jostled into the picture, laughing and waving. It felt a little nerve-racking knowing that we were going live to the nation and there wasn't a single human being at the controls!

I've spent most of my working life as a DJ and I've probably done as many Christmas Day shows as any living DJ. I used to love walking into Broadcasting House on Christmas Day. The commissionaires (receptionists to you and me) at the main entrance to the building are well known for their serious approach to their job but on Christmas Day even these professional custodians in their military-style uniforms ditched their customary reserve and waved us through with a grin and a festive greeting.

The streets outside were also unrecognizable from a normal day. All but a handful of shops, cafés, and bars were shut, there were no crowds, and anyone who happened to be out and about seemed to be in a generous mood, dispensing greetings to whoever was sharing the pavement with them. In that one day I used to exchange more nods and hellos with strangers than I would for the rest of the year. It was as if everyone had decided to take the day off being grumpy or suspicious. The next day they'd be barging you out of the way or telling you to get lost, but on Christmas Day it's all smiles and greetings. That's what I love about Christmas—the goodwill of strangers.

There is one Christmas Day broadcast I'll never forget. I was doing the morning show and I was talking live on air when the studio door opened and in walked a vicar ... wearing an enormous amount of makeup! He had come in to do the "Pause for Thought" slot, in which a representative of one of the major faiths is invited to deliver a short, reflective piece with a moral lesson in it for listeners to consider. They are generally pretty serious interludes in an otherwise lighthearted show, but I found myself really struggling not to dissolve into nervous hysterics as I introduced him and exchanged pleasantries over the airwaves. I couldn't work out what on earth he was doing, wearing makeup. It's moments like these that can ruin a DJ's reputation for professionalism! It's not every day I find myself broadcasting to millions, talking to a vicar made up as Ru Paul, but it was the shock and surrealism of it that set me off. He's called the Reverend Roger Royle, and I've since got to know him quite well. He's the world's loveliest, funniest vicar, and does lots of work for the BBC, including many of the funerals. Before delivering his piece, he explained about the makeup: he was appearing in [pantomime] somewhere up north, he told me, and hadn't had time to clean up; he had driven through the night like that to get to Broadcasting House.

LYNN PARSONS, disc jockey

# Will the Real Father Christmas Please Stand Up?

## The Origins of Santa Claus

ST. NICHOLAS IS PROBABLY THE most popular of the 10,000 or so saints venerated by Christians, and yet we know virtually nothing about him. There are more chapels and churches named after him than any of the 12 Apostles. Today, his name conjures up an image of a jolly *bon viveur* with a weakness for brandy and cakes, but the real St. Nicholas was nothing like his modern-day manifestation: he was a **pious, serious-minded, abstemious monk,** who shunned wealth and materialism and spent much of his life traveling the Middle East and helping the poor. There are all sorts of legends and tales about St. Nicholas, most of which are nonsense, but they have been repeated so often over the centuries, and in so many different recesses of the Christian Church, that some probably contain small elements of the truth. What we know for certain is that he was born at Parara, a city in Asia Minor (modern-day Turkey); he grew up in a wealthy family but gave away all the money he inherited; he made a pilgrimage to Egypt and Palestine as a young man; he was appointed Bishop of Myra, also in Asia Minor; he was imprisoned during the persecution of Christians under the Roman emperor Diocletian, and he was released after the accession of Constantine, famously the first emperor to convert to Christianity. He died on December 6 (his feast day) in AD 345 or 352. In 1087 Italian sailors stole his body from Myra and brought it back to the Italian port of Bari where he is now kept in the cathedral named after him. On his feast day, local sailors still carry his statue from the cathedral out to sea, in the hope that his blessing will protect them in the coming year.

Behold the maiestie and grace
of loueing. cheerfull, Christmas face.
Whome many thousands with one breath:
Cry out let him be put to death.
Who indeede can neuer die:
So long as man hath memory.

* * * *

BY THE START OF THE RENAISSANCE, NICHOLAS WAS WELL established as the **most popular saint** in Europe. Even after the Reformation, when Protestants sought to suppress the veneration of saints and other icons, his popularity remained undimmed, especially in the Netherlands. It was there that "Sinter Klaas" began his slow transformation from austere Asian monk into the jovial figure from the North Pole we recognize today. Early depictions of St. Nicholas show him wearing long flowing robes, sometimes in red, which perhaps explains how "Santa" came to acquire his characteristic red suit.

* * * *

*You know you're getting old when Santa starts looking younger.*

ANONYMOUS

ST. NICHOLAS IS THE PATRON SAINT OF DOZENS OF GROUPS OF
people, as well as several countries, cities, and towns. Those claiming the
benefit of the great man's patronage include scholars, sailors, merchants,
Russians, bakers, Greeks, pawnbrokers, archers, Neapolitans, bankers,
jurists, Sicilians, brewers, coopers, travelers, perfumers, unmarried girls,
brides, and robbers. But it is with young children, of whom he is also the
patron saint, that he has been most closely connected over the centuries,
although there is no hard evidence of a reason for this association,
only ludicrous legends. Perhaps the best known is the story of the three
impecunious daughters (see page 91) whom he rescues from a life of
penury by hurling money down their chimneys and straight into their
socks as he speeds by their house on his white steed. Another story to leave
you stammering in incredulity is the one about him bringing back to life
three young boys murdered by an innkeeper, who kept them, for reasons
unclear, in a barrel of brine. But there are so many of these tales that it's
safe to assume there's a sound historical basis to his reputation as someone
who was jolly nice to children.

❋ ❋ ❋ ❋

*There's nothing sadder in this world than to awake on
Christmas morning and not be a child.*

ERMA BOMBECK (1927–1996), American humorist

THE NOTION OF ST. NICHOLAS AS THE STEALTHY MIDNIGHT deliverer of gifts appears to have begun in the Netherlands in the late Middle Ages, but it was on the morning of December 6, his feast day, that he crept into homes to reward deserving children with presents, and undeserving ones with lumps of coal. When Christmas underwent its dramatic revival in the nineteenth century, the St. Nicholas delivery date, in the United States and Britain at least, switched to **Christmas Eve**. No one officially declared that Christmas Eve was stocking-filling night—it just evolved that way, probably because Victorian common sense and practical considerations dictated that it was neater to condense the St. Nicholas Day/Advent/Christmas/New Year holidays into a shorter period of time. Hardworking American settlers, grafting Victorian industrialists, and empire-builders could hardly be expected to give over the better part of a month to recreation and relaxation.

❋ ❋ ❋ ❋

THE PROTESTANT REFORMATION produced a rival to St. Nicholas in the form of the **Christkind** ("Christ Child") or Kris Kringle, as he became known in the United States. The Christkind is thought to be a German creation (some claim the idea came from Martin Luther himself) to discourage the Catholic habit of venerating saints like Nicholas. The Christkind is an angel-like figure, who, like St. Nicholas, delivers presents to worthy children. In Scandinavia, meanwhile, for centuries parents have been telling children that jolly elves, trolls, and gnomes deliver the gifts in a sleigh, drawn by goats or reindeer.

FATHER CHRISTMAS IS NOT just the British name for Santa Claus; he is a fictional character who emerges from the late medieval period, whose true origins may even pre-date Christianity. The American Santa Claus has one principal source of origin: the Dutch settlers who brought their veneration of Sinter Klaas with them to the New World. But in Britain, the modern-day character of Father Christmas is an amalgamation of Sinter Klaas and a more mysterious, uncertain figure from Norse and other pagan mythology, dating back to heaven only knows when, and bound up with the winter solstice and the coming of spring. Typically, he wore a long, hooded cloak and was festooned with evergreen wreaths of holly, ivy, or mistletoe. In Britain, he would be recognized as a version of the **Green Man**. But the existence of this pagan character is disputed by some historians, who point out that there is not a shred of hard evidence to support him. Some even claim paganists invented him in the last 200 years or so to add weight to the canon of their beliefs.

Supporters of the pagan Father Christmas theory say that his story, like other pagan characters and customs, has been passed down the years through the oral tradition from a time when the only writings were those produced by a handful of monks concentrating exclusively on the Christian experience.

❄ ❄ ❄ ❄

THE REINDEER IS VITALLY important to the **nomadic tribes** of the Arctic regions, especially the Lapps. The only deer that can be domesticated provides fat, meat, cheese, clothing, footwear, tools, and transport. The antlers and bones are used to make the tools and the sinews are used to make highly durable bindings.

❄ ❄ ❄ ❄

CENTURIES OF HUNTING AND THE gradual **destruction of its natural habitat** by man—much of it through the construction of hydroelectric power plants—

have combined to cause major problems for reindeer in the Arctic. The lands on which they have roamed for millennia have shrunk in size, the migration routes have been disrupted, and their population has dropped sharply.

❄ ❄ ❄ ❄

IN DAYS GONE BY, FINNS USED to measure distance by the length a reindeer can run without having to pee. The measurement is known as *poronkusema*, which, no surprises, means "reindeer pissing" and is thought to cover a distance of between 7 and 10 kilometers. Reindeer cannot pee while they're moving.

❄ ❄ ❄ ❄

THERE IS NO LAND BENEATH THE Arctic ice cap covering the North Pole, unlike its equivalent in the southern hemisphere. The sea ice is between 2 and 3 meters thick, and its total area halves in size during the summer months. In 2004, an international team of 300 scientists published an alarming report into the impact of global warming on the Arctic ice pack, which, they claim, will reduce by as much as 50 percent by the end of the century. The **big meltdown** will cause sea levels to rise so high they will flood many low-lying lands around the world, and they may even alter the currents of the oceans and regional climates.

❄ ❄ ❄ ❄

THERE ARE EIGHTY PEOPLE listed in the telephone directory across the United States under the name S. Claus.

❄ ❄ ❄ ❄

A DAY-OLD REINDEER CALF CAN outsprint a man.

❄ ❄ ❄ ❄

REINDEER ARE THE ONLY SPECIES of deer in which the **females have horns**—an evolutionary quirk that helps them compete with males for the meager food supplies in their harsh environment.

THE FIRST WRITTEN REFERENCES to the pagan Father Christmas figure begin to surface in the 1400s, where he appears frequently in the traditional mummers' plays performed in England over the Christmas period. A fifteenth-century carol includes the line "Welcome, my lord Christmas." In Tudor and Stuart times he is referred to as Sir Christmas, Captain Christmas, or Old Christmas. Whatever his name or guise, Christmas was always **cheerful, generous, amusing, overweight, and bearded**. The first image of Father Christmas comes in 1638 in the form of an illustration by writer Thomas Nabbes, who depicted him as an old man in a furred coat and cap. When the Puritans banned Christmas celebrations in the mid-seventeenth century, Father Christmas "went dark," as the spies say, and emerged as a powerful allegorical figure, representing the outlawed festivities and mocking the new authorities.

❋ ❋ ❋ ❋

IT WAS DURING THE EARLY NINETEENTH CENTURY THAT ST. NICHOLAS and Father Christmas began to merge into the Santa Claus character we recognize today. **Dutch settlers** on the eastern seaboard of the United States, most notably in New York, made something of a public show of celebrating St. Nicholas's feast day on December 6, and there are a number of engravings from that time showing the saint in a hat and robes, with images of stockings full of gifts and fruit hung at the fireside. It was, however, still very much an exclusively Dutch tradition to which no one else, bar a handful of satirists, paid much attention.

❋ ❋ ❋ ❋

SANTA CLAUS WASN'T BORN, HE EVOLVED, BUT IF WE HAD TO GIVE HIM a birthday it would be December 23, 1822. The man responsible for introducing the Santa we recognize today into the heart of the Western Christmas experience was a strait-laced Episcopalian minister and classical scholar called **Clement Clark Moore**. Little could Moore have known at the time that his fame would be based, not on any of his lifetime labors, but on a piece of borderline doggerel, which he dashed off, half asleep, before retiring to bed one night. Until then, Moore was best known for a hefty two-volume work titled *A Compendious Lexicon of the Hebrew Language*.

The New York professor supposedly wrote his famous poem, "An Account of a Visit from St. Nicholas," on the evening of the 23rd and read it to his three daughters the following night, just a few hours before St. Nick and the eight reindeer he depicted parked up on the family roof. Thus, with a blast of imaginative thinking and a few strokes of his pen, the professor transformed an ascetic Turkish monk into a **fat, slightly camp old man** with a dubious dress sense and a whiff of brandy on his beard, blessed with the extraordinary ability to traverse the globe in a single day, flying from house to house in a sleigh drawn by reindeer, descending chimneys and dispensing gifts to good children throughout the Christian world. It was fortunate perhaps that the serious-minded and austere St. Nicholas was no longer alive to witness his extraordinary transformation. A woman friend of the Moore family liked the poem so much that she sent a copy to the *Troy Sentinel* newspaper, who published it the following year. The fact that it was published anonymously has provided the basis for some not very convincing conspiracy theories that Moore was not the poem's author. (It was John F. Kennedy, apparently.) In truth, Moore was a respected scholar with a reputation to uphold, who was probably trying to distance himself from such a frivolous piece of work.

❋ ❋ ❋ ❋

IN THE 1860S, THOMAS NAST, THE FATHER OF AMERICAN POLITICAL cartooning, produced a string of famous illustrations inspired by Moore's poem that succeeded in entrenching Santa's image in the mind of the public. Published in the popular *Harper's Weekly*, the illustrations depict a **short, almost troll-like figure**, with a full white beard, portly frame and fur-trimmed suit, clutching a pile of toys under his arm with a sack on his back and a pipe in his mouth. But for a handful of modifications, the image of Santa Claus has changed remarkably little in almost 150 years. His long pipe has been lost over the years to the forces of political correctness and he's grown a few inches over the decades, but otherwise Nast's likeness is one that we would recognize today. A famous Coca-Cola ad from 1931 once and for all established red as the standard color for Father Christmas's suit. The illustrator Haddon Sundblum also added a black belt and black boots.

'Twas the night before Christmas, when all through the house
Not a creature was stirring, not even a mouse.
The stockings were hung by the chimney with care,
In hopes that St. Nicholas soon would be there.
The children were nestled all snug in their beds,
While visions of sugar-plums danced through their heads,
And mamma in her kerchief, and I in my cap,
Had just settled our brains for a long winter's nap,
When out on the lawn there arose such a clatter,
I sprang from the bed to see what was the matter.
Away to the window I flew like a flash,
Tore open the shutters and threw up the sash.
The moon, on the breast of the new-fallen snow
Gave a luster of midday to objects below;
When, what to my wondering eyes should appear,
But a miniature sleigh, and eight tiny reindeer.
With a little old driver, so lively and quick,
I knew in a moment it must be St. Nick.
More rapid than eagles his coursers they came,
And he whistled, and shouted, and called them by name!
"Now Dasher! now, Dancer! now, Prancer and Vixen!
On, Comet! On, Cupid! on, on, Donner and Blitzen!
To the top of the porch! to the top of the wall!
Now dash away! Dash away! Dash away all!"
As dry leaves that before the wild hurricane fly,
When they meet with an obstacle, mount to the sky,
So up to the house-top the coursers they flew,
With a sleigh full of toys, and St. Nicholas too.

And then, in a twinkling, I heard on the roof
The prancing and pawing of each little hoof.
As I drew in my head, and was turning around,
Down the chimney St. Nicholas came with a bound.
He was dressed all in fur, from his head to his foot,
And his clothes were all tarnished with ashes and soot.
A bundle of toys he had flung on his back,
And he looked like a peddler, just opening his pack.
His eyes—how they twinkled! his dimples how merry!
His cheeks were like roses, his nose like a cherry!
His droll little mouth was drawn up like a bow,
And the beard of his chin was as white as the snow.
The stump of a pipe he held tight in his teeth,
And the smoke it encircled his head like a wreath.
He had a broad face and a little round belly,
That shook when he laughed, like a bowlful of jelly.
He was chubby and plump, a right jolly old elf,
And I laughed when I saw him, in spite of myself!
A wink of his eye and a twist of his head,
Soon gave me to know I had nothing to dread.
He spoke not a word, but went straight to his work,
And filled all the stockings; then turned with a jerk,
And laying his finger aside of his nose,
And giving a nod, up the chimney he rose!
He sprang to his sleigh, to his team gave a whistle,
And away they all flew like the down of a thistle.
But I heard him exclaim, 'ere he drove out of sight,
"Happy Christmas to all, and to all a good-night!"

CLEMENT CLARK MOORE (1779–1863), "An Account of a Visit from St. Nicholas"

MOORE'S POEM HAS spawned scores of parodies, many of them very clever, some obscene, but most just plain silly. Writing them and circulating them on the web, or by email, has become something of an American Christmas custom in its own right. Below and on page 142 are two of the more amusing ones:

## The Night Before Christmas, Legally Speaking

*Whereas, on or about the night prior to Christmas, there did occur at a certain improved piece of real property (hereinafter "the House") a general lack of stirring by all creatures therein, including, but not limited to, a mouse.*

*A variety of foot apparel, e.g., stocking, socks, etc., had been affixed by and around the chimney in said House in the hope and/or belief that St. Nick aka St. Nicholas aka Santa Claus (hereinafter "Claus") would arrive at sometime thereafter.*

*The minor residents, i.e., the children, of the aforementioned House were located in their individual beds and were engaged in nocturnal*

*hallucinations, i.e., dreams, wherein vision of confectionery treats, including, but not limited to, candies, nuts and/or sugar plums, did dance, cavort, and otherwise appear in said dreams.*

*Whereupon the party of the first part (sometimes hereinafter referred to as "I"), being the joint-owner in fee simple of the House with the party of the second part (hereinafter "Mamma"), and said Mamma had retired for a sustained period of sleep. (At such time, the parties were clad in various forms of headgear, e.g., kerchief and cap.)*

*Suddenly, and without prior notice or warning, there did occur upon the unimproved real property adjacent and appurtenant to said House, i.e., the lawn, a certain disruption of unknown nature, cause, and/or circumstance. The party of the first part did immediately rush to a window in the House to investigate the cause of such disturbance.*

*At that time, the party of the first part did observe, with some degree of wonder and/or disbelief, a miniature sleigh (hereinafter "the Vehicle") being pulled and/or drawn very rapidly through the air by approximately eight (8) reindeer. The driver of the Vehicle* appeared to be and in fact was, the previously referenced Claus.

Said Claus was providing specific direction, instruction, and guidance to the approximately eight (8) reindeer and specifically identified the animal co-conspirators by name: Dasher, Dancer, Prancer, Vixen, Comet, Cupid, Donner, and Blitzen (hereinafter "the Deer"). (Upon information and belief, it is further asserted that an additional co-conspirator named "Rudolph" may have been involved.)

The party of the first part witnessed Claus, the Vehicle, and the Deer intentionally and willfully trespass upon the roofs of several residences located adjacent to and in the vicinity of the House, and noted that the Vehicle was heavily laden with packages, toys, and other items of unknown origin or nature. Suddenly, without prior invitation or permission, either express or implied, the Vehicle arrived at the House, and Claus entered said House via the chimney.

Said Claus was clad in a red fur suit, which was partially covered with residue from the chimney, and he carried a large sack containing a portion of the aforementioned packages, toys, and other unknown items. He was smoking what appeared to be tobacco in a small pipe in blatant violation

of local ordinances and health regulations.

Claus did not speak, but immediately began to fill the stocking of the minor children, which hung adjacent to the chimney, with toys and other small gifts. (Said items did not, however, constitute "gifts" to said minors pursuant to the applicable provisions of the U.S. Tax Code.)

Upon completion of such task, Claus touched the side of his nose and flew, rose, and/or ascended up the chimney of the House to the roof where the Vehicle and Deer waited and/or served as "lookouts." Claus immediately departed for an unknown destination.

However, prior to the departure of the Vehicle, Deer, and Claus from said House, the party of the first part did hear Claus state and/or exclaim: "Merry Christmas to all and to all a good night!" Or words to that effect.

AUTHOR UNKNOWN

❄ ❄ ❄ ❄

The one thing women don't want to find in their stockings on Christmas morning is their husband.

JOAN RIVERS (1933– )
American comedian

## The Cat Before Christmas

*'Twas the night before Christmas and all through the house*
*Not a creature was stirring, not even a mouse.*
*Cos the cat had pounced on him and tore him apart*
*Ate his mousey intestines and chewed up his heart.*
*Kitty thought he heard sleigh bells, which made him take pause*
*He stopped daintily licking the blood from his claws.*
*"Must be Santa," thought Kitty, that quite clever cat*
*"Cos nobody else climbs down the chimney like that."*
*Indeed it was ol' Santa, so jolly and fat*
*With a load of presents, and all for the cat!*
*"Wow, the best Christmas ever!" Kitty thought with a purr,*
*Then he coughed up a hairball and shed some more fur.*

AUTHOR UNKNOWN

❄ ❄ ❄ ❄

RUDOLPH, THE MOST FAMOUS REINDEER OF ALL, ENTERED THE
world more than a century after Clement Clark Moore gave us
Dasher, Dancer, Prancer, and Vixen. The shy one with the **bright
red nose**, who showed the world that a facial abnormality is no
bar to career advancement or a happy life, was the brainchild of
American copywriter Robert L. May. He came up with the Rudolph
narrative poem in 1939 as a way of attracting more customers into
the Montgomery Ward chain of department stores. The poem
sold more than two million copies that year and when it was
republished in 1946, after World War II, the book
sold another 3.5 million.

❄ ❄ ❄ ❄

DEPARTMENT STORE SANTA CLAUSES WITH
real white bushy beards earn up to twice
as much as their colleagues with imitation
beards.

NEVER TRUST A MAN WITH A BEARD, THEY SAY ... ER, EXCEPT SANTA Claus. **Fear of facial hair** (other people's) is a surprisingly common phobia affecting the health and lifestyle of thousands of people around the world, according to experts. Pogonophobia is defined as "a persistent, abnormal, and unwarranted fear of beards" that apparently can cause profound distress to sufferers. (You can only imagine the suffering of pogonophobes in Victorian times—the Golden Age of the Beard—especially if they were soldiers serving in beard-crazy Afghanistan or the Punjab. There can't have been a clean-shaven face for hundreds of miles!) The CTRN Phobia Clinic is an American organization that claims to have helped presidents, royals, celebrities, and top sportsmen overcome their phobias. (CTRN stands for "Change That's Right Now.") Reading the company's literature, it becomes clear that pogonophobia is not something we should be chuckling into our beards about at all, in fact. Read this and you will never laugh about facial hair again:

*... the problem often significantly impacts the quality of life. It can cause panic attacks and keep people apart from loved ones and business associates. Symptoms typically include shortness of breath, rapid breathing, irregular heartbeat, sweating, nausea, and overall feelings of dread, although everyone experiences pogonophobia in their own way and may have different symptoms. Though a variety of potent drugs are often prescribed for pogonophobia, side effects and/or withdrawal symptoms can be severe. Moreover, drugs do not "cure" pogonophobia or any other phobia. At best they temporarily suppress the symptoms through chemical interaction....*

*If you are living with pogonophobia, what is the real cost to your health, your career or school, and to your family life? Avoiding the issue indefinitely would mean resigning yourself to living in fear, missing out on priceless life experiences big and small, living a life that is just a shadow of what it will be when the problem is gone.*

*For anyone earning a living, the financial toll of this phobia is incalculable. Living with fear means you can never concentrate fully and give your best. Lost opportunities. Poor performance or grades. Promotions that pass you by. Pogonophobia will likely cost you tens, even hundreds of thousands of dollars over the course of your lifetime, let alone the cost to your health and quality of life. Like all fears and phobias, pogonophobia is created by the unconscious mind as a protective mechanism. At some point in your past, there was likely an event linking beards and emotional trauma. While the original catalyst may have been a real-life scare of some kind, the condition can also be triggered by myriad benign events like movies, TV, or perhaps seeing someone else experience trauma.*

IF SANTA'S SLEIGH WAS LOADED WITH ONE BARBIE DOLL AND ONE action figure for every girl and boy on the planet it would weigh **400,000 tons** and need almost a billion reindeer to pull it. To deliver all his presents in one global night-time, Santa would have to deliver to roughly 1,500 homes a second and, allowing for chimney descents and cookie breaks, he and the reindeer would have to travel at roughly 5,000 times the speed of sound. I understand from my contacts in the aviation industry that aircraft would burst into flames at just a fraction of that speed.

❄ ❄ ❄ ❄

THE FOLLOWING WAS FIRST PRINTED ON THE EDITORIAL PAGE OF THE *New York Sun* newspaper on September 21, 1897, under the headline: **"Yes, Virginia, There Is a Santa Claus!"**

*We take pleasure in answering thus prominently the communication below, expressing at the same time our great gratification that its faithful author is numbered among the friends of* The Sun:

*"I am 8 years old. Some of my little friends say there is no Santa Claus. Papa says, 'If you see it in* The Sun, *it's so.' Please tell me the truth, is there a Santa Claus?" Virginia O'Hanlon*

*Virginia, your little friends are wrong. They have been affected by the scepticism of a sceptical age. They do not believe except for what they see. They think that nothing can be which is not comprehensible by their little minds. All minds, Virginia, whether they be men's or children's, are little. In this great universe of ours, man is a mere insect, an ant, in his intellect as compared with the boundless world about him, as measured by the intelligence capable of grasping the whole of truth and knowledge.*

*Yes, Virginia, there is a Santa Claus.*

*He exists as certainly as love and generosity and devotion exist, and you know that they abound and give to your life its highest beauty and joy. Alas! How dreary would be the world if there were no Santa Claus! It would be as dreary as if there were no Virginias. There would be no childlike faith then, no poetry, no romance to make tolerable this existence. We should have no enjoyment, except in sense and sight. The external light with which childhood fills the world would be extinguished.*

*Not believe in Santa Claus! You might as well not believe in fairies. You might get your papa to hire men to watch in all the chimneys on Christmas eve to catch Santa Claus, but even if you did not see Santa Claus coming down, what would that prove? Nobody sees Santa Claus, but that is no sign that there is no Santa Claus. The most real things in the world are those that neither children nor* men can see. Did you ever see fairies dancing on the lawn? Of course not, but that's no proof that they are not there. Nobody can conceive or imagine all the wonders there are unseen and unseeable in the world.

You tear apart the baby's rattle and see what makes the noise inside, but there is a veil covering the unseen world which not the strongest man, nor even the united strength of all the strongest men that ever lived could tear apart. Only faith, poetry, love, romance, can push aside that curtain and view and picture the supernatural beauty and glory beyond. Is it all real? Ah, Virginia, in all this world there is nothing else real and abiding.

No Santa Claus? Thank God he lives and lives forever. A thousand years from now, Virginia, nay 10 times 10,000 years from now, he will continue to make glad the heart of childhood.

Merry Christmas and a Happy New Year!

# THE FIREFIGHTER

WHEN I WAS YOUNG AND HAD NO CHILDREN I USED TO LOVE WORKING the Christmas Day shift. You got double money and there was often some overtime to be had because in those days there were always call-outs at Christmas, generally later in the day when people had had a few drinks and got a bit careless. Today, thanks to our emphasis on education and the installation of more and more smoke alarms, we don't get called out nearly as often. Most of the single firefighters on the brigade, or those without children, used to volunteer to work the day so that the men and women with young families could be at home. In fairness, it was no great sacrifice because there was always a party atmosphere at the station on the day shift.

It seems incredible now but when I joined the Fire Brigade, in the early 1980s, we used to cook up a full turkey lunch with all the trimmings and even the odd bottle of wine or beer. I was looking through some old photo albums recently and was amazed by the pictures I took on Christmas Day 1985, when I was stationed at Ealing in West London. The entire crew were sitting around the table with paper hats on their heads, grinning from ear to ear at the end of what was clearly a highly enjoyable occasion. There were streamers all round the room, two bottles of wine and a few cans of beer on the table, and a pile of plates and turkey bones scattered across the surfaces. Such a scene is unimaginable today because our working practices have changed beyond all recognition. For a start, we no longer have the extensive kitchen facilities of old with which to cook a full Christmas feast—at least that's the case in the Staffordshire fire service and I believe it's a similar situation up and down the country. Nowadays people tend to bring in packed lunches, which we generally eat watching TV rather than congregating around a long table as we once did. There are no longer any beds either, so if you're working the night shift, you have to rest—or try to—on the reclining seats that have recently been provided for us.

Christmas Day is still one of the few Bank Holidays we get, but it's not so much fun these days. In truth, it's just like any other day, a bit depressing even, because you know that your family, and almost everybody else out there, are all at home enjoying themselves. I have three young children of my own now and if I have to work on Christmas Day I prefer to work the day shift, so at least I get to be with them when they tear open their stockings at first light. Watching their joy and excitement is the high point of the day for me. If possible I try not to work overnight on Christmas Eve because that means I don't get back home until mid-morning. If it's been a busy night I'll also be very tired, which isn't great given how busy it gets at home on Christmas Day.

It's a shame that working at Christmas is no longer the boisterous, happy affair it used to be. Apart from the sheer fun of it, you felt a powerful sense of camaraderie with the rest of the crew as we crowded around the table, bantering and making speeches and toasts. In hindsight, I suppose it's remarkable that we were ever allowed to drink on the premises and it was no surprise when they quickly began to phase out alcohol in stations the year after I took that photograph of our Christmas lunch—a ruling hastened by a drink-drive incident involving a firefighter in one of the London crews. Like us at Ealing, his crew had enjoyed a traditional Christmas lunch but when they were called out later in the day the driver of one of the engines must have been a little ragged around the edges and managed to crash, first into a pharmacy and then into a parked car, provoking a furious response from the car's owner. The pharmacy was located at the bottom of a block of apartments and all the occupants of the building had to be evacuated amid fears for its structural safety. To make matters worse, the driver ran away and when police later caught up with him at home, he was Breathalyzed and found to be twice the old legal limit, although he claimed that he only started drinking *after* the crash. It being a quiet day for news, the incident found its way into the headlines of the national newspapers.

The great majority of us, however, were very sensible about drinking on Christmas Day, not least because we spend much of our working lives attending to fires, crashes, and incidents that have been caused by alcohol, but some crews had a reputation for enjoying their drink more than others. It was reasonable and inevitable to ban drinking on the job and, in the wider scheme of things, missing out on a traditional Christmas lunch is, I suppose, a small hardship to bear. Today, each of the four crews has a Christmas "office party" at a restaurant, just like everyone else, but somehow it's not quite the same.

RANDLE WILBRAHAM
Staffordshire Fire and Rescue Service

# Moon Orbits, Tsunamis, and Train Crashes

## News Stories That Shook Christmas

AT 7:15 P.M. ON December 28, 1879, the newly constructed **Tay Bridge** at Dundee, Scotland, collapsed into the river below during a severe storm, taking with it a six-carriage train with approximately 75 passengers on board. There were no survivors. At just over two miles in length, the Tay was the longest bridge in the world at the time, and its construction provoked great excitement in Victorian society. Designed by Thomas Bouch, who was knighted for his efforts, the bridge took six years to build and was opened, amid great fanfare, in May 1878. Six hundred laborers, twenty of whom died in the construction, used over 10 million bricks and 2 million rivets to build it. Investigations into the collapse laid the blame on Bouch's poor design. The tragedy caused an outpouring of grief and shock across the country and was responsible for what many people regard as the worst well-known poem in the English language, written by the world's worst poet, William McGonagall. The simple title "The Tay Bridge Disaster" gives no indication of the poetic horrors that follow. Doctors recommend that only small passages of the poem be read at a time, so below I have laid out merely the first and last stanzas for your enjoyment. Deep breaths now.

*Beautiful railway bridge of the Silv'ry Tay!*
*Alas! I am very sorry to say*
*That ninety lives have been taken away*
*On the last Sabbath day of 1879,*
*Which will be remember'd for a very long time....*

*It must have been an awful sight,*
*To witness in the dusky moonlight,*
*While the Storm Fiend did laugh, and angry did bray,*
*Along the Railway Bridge of the Silv'ry Tay,*
*Oh! ill-fated Bridge of the Silv'ry Tay,*
*I must now conclude my lay*
*By telling the world fearlessly without the least dismay,*
*That your central girders would not have given way,*
*At least many sensible men do say,*
*Had they been supported on each side with buttresses,*
*At least many sensible men confesses,*
*For the stronger we our houses do build,*
*The less chance we have of being killed.*

❄ ❄ ❄ ❄

ON DECEMBER 26, 1908, AMERICAN BOXER JACK JOHNSON STRUCK a blow for racial equality when he became the first black heavyweight world champion by knocking out Canadian Tommy Burns in the fourteenth round of their fight in Sydney, Australia. Johnson had followed Burns all over the world, demanding a contest and taunting him in the press. The fight was stopped by the police after Johnson had handed out a severe beating to his opponent. Ever controversial, Johnson—the most famous black man on the planet for two decades—goaded Burns and his ringside team throughout the bout. Barely anyone in the 20,000-strong crowd cheered the American as he dominated Burns. Each time Burns looked like he was going to collapse, Johnson held him up so that he could hammer him more. Johnson, who received a tepid welcome on his return to the United States, had defeated a string of challengers to keep his title when, in 1910, he came face to face with Jim Jeffries, the Great White Hope. Jeffries came out of retirement to try to beat the controversial and flamboyant Johnson. During the contest at Reno, Nevada, Johnson became the first boxer to knock down Jeffries, whose corner threw in the towel in the fifteenth round. Johnson's victory triggered racial violence and rioting across the United States.

On December 28, 1908, Italy was in the middle of its long Christmas holidays when **the worst earthquake** in European history, followed by a giant tsunami, brought immeasurable devastation to the south of the country. Hundreds of buildings collapsed when the quake struck the Messina Strait which separates Calabria from Sicily, at 5:30 in the morning. Tens of thousands were entombed in their homes as they slept, while many others were killed by falling buildings as they fled into the streets. Estimates of the death toll vary but most agree that the figure was not less than 200,000. The towns of Messina (population 150,000) and Reggio Calabria (50,000), the biggest in the region, were razed to the ground by a quake that would measure roughly 7.5 on the modern Richter scale.

❅ ❅ ❅ ❅

France's worst peacetime railway disaster took place two days before Christmas in 1933 when the country's largest locomotive, traveling at over 60 mph, rammed into the rear of a stationary train standing at Lagny-Pomponne station, 17 miles from Paris. The **horrendous crash**, which killed 238 people and injured over 300, was blamed on the driver of the Strasbourg express, who ignored several signals in a bid to make up lost time. Such was the impact of the collision that many of the wooden coaches were reduced to splinters. The giant locomotive was later repaired and returned to service, and was dubbed **"Le Charcutier"** (the butcher) by dry-witted railway engineers. The worst rail disaster of the twentieth century had also happened in France, in 1917, when a military train derailed as it headed into a tunnel in the Alps. Officially, 540 people died, but other estimates suggest the figure was closer to 800.

❋ ❋ ❋ ❋

NEW ZEALAND WAS PLUNGED into mourning on Christmas Eve 1953 when a flood triggered by minor volcanic activity swept away a train on a bridge. One hundred and fifty of the 285 passengers on board, most of them **en route to see Queen Elizabeth II** during her first state visit to the country, died when six of the nine carriages sank to the bottom of the flooded Whangaehu River. In a bizarre sequence of events, the volcanic Mount Ruapehu on the North Island experienced a small eruption, releasing millions of gallons of water from a lake that surged down the mountainside before crashing into the bridge. Destabilized by the torrent of water, the bridge collapsed when the Wellington to Auckland express train crossed it minutes later. Arthur Cyril Ellis, a local postal clerk, tried to warn the approaching train by running down the line and waving his torch. The driver applied the brakes but the train was too close to the bridge.

ON CHRISTMAS EVE 1968 the three astronauts of the Apollo 8 spacecraft became the first manned space mission to orbit the moon. Watched live by a global television audience, the Americans fired their rocket engine to send Apollo 8 into the first of 10 elliptical lunar orbits. For 45 minutes of each orbit, Apollo 8 passed out of contact with mission control in Houston when it disappeared to the **dark side of the moon**, which had never previously been seen by man. During the orbits, the astronauts—Frank Borman, James Lovell, and William Anders—sent back the television pictures of what they were seeing. They also quoted from the Book of Genesis, describing the creation of the world. The astronauts struggled to sleep during the three-day voyage, complaining that as they could not rest their heads in the weightless atmosphere they kept jerking themselves awake, thinking that they were falling. Early in the flight, Borman fell sick, vomiting twice and suffering a bout of diarrhea, which filled the spacecraft with globules of vomit and feces. On Christmas Day the astronauts opened their food lockers to discover a meal of real turkey with stuffing and three miniature bottles of brandy, together with some presents from their wives. After splashing down in the Pacific on December 27 they were picked up by the aircraft carrier *Yorktown* and returned to the United States as national heroes.

❄ ❄ ❄ ❄

DEATH, DESTRUCTION, CIVIL UNREST, AND DISEASE VISITED THE Nicaraguan capital of Managua during the Christmas holiday period of 1972 after a 6.2-magnitude earthquake killed 10,000 people and left a quarter of a million homeless. Three-quarters of the city was destroyed when the earthquake struck in the dead of night, wiping out all electricity, gas, water, sewage, and telephone systems in a matter of seconds. **The tremors continued for hours** as hundreds of fires broke out across the capital, which was built on poor soil over four significant fault lines. With thousands of dead and dying left under the rubble, President Somoza Debyale ordered an immediate evacuation of the city and the imposition of martial law as chaos erupted. Four major hospitals were destroyed in the quake, leaving thousands of casualties without medical treatment. Bodies were burned in the streets to prevent the spread of disease. In the clean-up operation, most of the city was bulldozed with the bodies of the dead still in the rubble.

❄ ❄ ❄ ❄

CHRISTMAS JOY TURNED TO DESPAIR FOR THE CITIZENS OF DARWIN when **Cyclone Tracy** reduced the Australian city to rubble on December 25, 1974. Incredibly, only 65 people were killed in one of the country's worst natural disasters, even though 9,000 homes and 90 percent of the city were destroyed in the raging storm. Thousands of people were left homeless after winds touching 140 mph and torrential rain crashed into the country's northern coast. In the week following Christmas Day, over 25,000 people were flown out of the city and a further 10,000 escaped by road, leaving a population of just 10,000 amid the ruins and floodwater.

THE CORNISH FISHING COMMUNITY OF **MOUSEHOLE** SPENT CHRISTMAS 1981 in mourning after eight local lifeboatmen were drowned answering an emergency call in a violent storm. The crew of the *Solomon Browne* launched in a Force-12 (Category 5) hurricane with winds gusting at almost 100 knots and waves towering as high as sixty feet. Many of the crew had been socializing in the British Legion club when the distress signal was received, and conditions were so bad that it was decided only one volunteer from each family should go. The RNLI boat was attempting to assist the stricken *Union Star*, which was being driven toward the rocky coastline to a certain destruction. There were eight people aboard the coaster—on her maiden voyage from Denmark to Ireland—including the captain's pregnant wife and his two stepdaughters. Reports suggested that the lifeboatmen, at huge risk to their own lives, had managed to rescue four people when disaster struck. The following morning, searchers found the lifeboat smashed into small pieces against the cliffs, while the *Union Star* had been flipped upside down and was stuck on the rocks. Posthumous awards were made to the lifeboat crew for what was regarded as exceptional gallantry, even by the high standards of the RNLI.

ON DECEMBER 17, 1983, ONE OF THE BUSIEST SHOPPING DAYS OF THE year, an IRA car bomb exploded outside **Harrods** department store in central London killing six people, including three policemen, and injuring 90. The area was packed with Christmas shoppers as the blast tore through the streets and filled the air with a cloud of black smoke.

BRITAIN SUFFERED ITS WORST TERRORIST OUTRAGE AND AVIATION disaster on December 21, 1988, when **Pan Am flight 103** was blown up over the Scottish border, killing all 259 people on board and 11 on the ground. The jumbo jet, en route to New York from London Heathrow, burst into flames at about 31,000 feet following the explosion of a bomb, planted in a suitcase by a Libyan secret agent. The wreckage

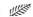
from the plane was littered over 800 square miles, though much of it rained down on the Scottish village of Lockerbie. The impact of the plane hitting the ground registered 1.6 on the Richter scale. The police investigation was the biggest ever mounted in Scotland.

❄ ❄ ❄ ❄

GERMANY HAD PLENTY TO CHEER ABOUT OVER CHRISTMAS 1989 after the Brandenburg Gate was opened for the first time in almost three decades on December 22, officially ending the bitter division between the east and west of the country. Tens of thousands of elated Germans took to the streets in driving rain to witness the ceremony at one of the most powerful symbols of Cold War division. West German Chancellor Helmut Kohl walked through a tunnel in the Gate to be greeted by Hans Modrow, the prime minister of East Germany. Minutes later the gates were opened and thousands of people poured across the old border, waving, kissing, and hugging each other, while others clambered on to the top of the Berlin Wall chanting, "Deutschland!" Addressing the enormous crowd, Kohl declared the historic occasion the "most important moment of my life."

❄ ❄ ❄ ❄

BY FAR THE WORST NATURAL DISASTER IN RECENT TIMES TOOK PLACE on December 26, 2004, when a **tsunami**, triggered by a powerful earthquake under the Indian Ocean, killed almost a quarter of a million in southern Asia. The 8.9-magnitude earthquake forced up a long section of the ocean floor by about 10 meters, creating an enormous sea surge that sent waves racing toward land at speeds touching 500 mph. The north Indonesian coast, close to the quake's epicenter, bore the brunt of the world's largest tsunami for 40 years when it crashed ashore, without any warning, in mid-morning. The giant body of water spread rapidly in all directions, devastating the resort coasts of Sri Lanka and Thailand and the fishing communities of southern India. The tsunami also caused deaths further afield in Malaysia, the Maldives, and the Seychelles and was even felt thousands of miles away on the east coast of Africa. Tens of thousands of people watched their loved ones being swept out to sea, and the bodies of many of the dead have never been found. The exact death toll will never be known but more than 200,000 people in 13 countries— roughly 130,000 in Indonesia—have been certified as dead or missing. The tragedy shocked the world, triggering a flood of grief and charity that led to the donation of over $15 billion to help with relief and reconstruction efforts.

# THE LIFEBOATMAN

I WASN'T MANNING THE STATION ON CHRISTMAS DAY BUT AS ALWAYS I WAS on call. Although there's plenty of commercial shipping going up and down the Channel, you don't expect many others to be out at sea. But just as I was settling down for a quiet end to the day the coastguard at Dover paged me; he had received a 999 call from someone on top of the cliffs at Beachy Head. The caller had been out walking his dog in the fading light when he heard voices shouting for help. He looked down from the cliff's edge and saw two people stuck on a ledge about halfway up the cliffs, which are about 500 feet high. It was clear that they had been cut off by the tides and had thought they could climb to safety. Right at the bottom the cliffs are not so steep. They suddenly become sheer, however, as this couple had discovered. They were lucky: it was almost dark when they were finally heard, and it was unlikely that anyone else would have come along later. Two local coastguard teams had gone up to the cliff tops in their Land Rovers, and decided it would be safest to winch a man down to the ledge. From there he could take them one by one down to an RNLI boat. The weather wasn't too bad, but the dark was sure to pose some problems.

The center of Eastbourne was very quiet when I drove off and it took me only about five minutes to travel the three miles to the station for the all-weather lifeboat. The inshore lifeboat is located nearer the town center and the crews for both had been paged at the same time as I had. There was a pretty impressive turnout considering it was Christmas Day. All eight crew for the all-weather boat, all six for the inshore boat, and 14 shore helpers were ready to get going within minutes of the alarm being raised. We all knew what to do. The training just kicks in. My job as coxswain is to drive the bigger, all-weather boat and take command of the operation at sea.

It took us about 20 minutes to get to Beachy Head, but the faster inshore boat had already located the stranded couple with their searchlights. Luckily the couple had brought a flashlight with them. There wasn't much we could do at first except stand clear and keep our powerful lights on them while the coastguard teams on the cliffs rigged up their winches. It's a fairly straightforward routine which involves digging spikes deep into the earth and then attaching rolling winches to them before lowering the man over.

What quickly became apparent was that the woman had slipped and tumbled about 60 feet down the nearly sheer slope before getting wedged in a gully. This was very, very lucky for her because if she had kept falling she wouldn't have survived. This realization increased the pressure on us because we didn't know if she had been injured. Either way, she would have been very badly shaken up. The good news was that we could see that both were wearing warm clothing. For some reason, I had been expecting the couple to be very young. I was a little surprised to discover they were in their fifties.

We kept one of our lights trained on the coastguard as he was winched down to the woman, attached his harness to her, and then continued down to the foot of the cliffs. The smaller inshore lifeboat was waiting at the water's edge to collect her and bring her over to us, before returning to pick up her partner. As they were lifted aboard you could tell both of them had been very frightened, but there was a huge sense of relief too. The woman confessed that the worst part of the whole experience was the seasickness she had begun to feel while waiting on the boat! "Well, there's just no pleasing some people is there?" joked one of the lads in the crew. "You pluck someone off a cliff ledge and the next thing they're moaning about the motion of the rescue boat!"

"Merry Christmas!" one of the crew members said as he pulled the man aboard. "Bah humbug, more like!" he replied. We wrapped them both up in thick blankets and gave them a cup of hot tea as we began to make our way home. By five o'clock we were back at the station, which was pretty impressive considering that just 90 minutes earlier we had all been snoozing in our armchairs or digging into our turkey roast. It was a good team effort. A paramedic checked the couple over before we dropped them back at their car, and they were able to drive home to London. We don't see it as our role to lecture people about their behavior, and so we just wished the couple well and went on our way. The coastguard, though, gently commented that they might have been better off waiting a short while for the tide to turn rather than climbing a 500-foot cliff in the gathering darkness. By half past six I was back home, just in time to settle down with the kids and watch *Ghostbusters*.

MARK SAWYER, RNLI

# Turkey Kebabs and Steamed Goldfish

## Christmas Customs around the World

THE CELEBRATION OF CHRISTMAS, such a joyful event in medieval times, was virtually killed off by the English Puritans, together with their emigrant cousins in North America, and it took the better part of two centuries for it to recover. Until Victoria married Prince Albert and Dickens picked up his quill, December 25 remained a day of quiet religious observation; the once-boisterous celebrations of the twelve-day holiday season were no more than tales of a distant past. For the majority of other Christian cultures around the world, however, this was how it ever was—and continued to be, even following the sensational and sudden revival of Christmas in Britain and the United States in the mid-nineteenth century. The two countries were the most powerful and influential in the world in the second half of that century, and their cultures inevitably filtered into others around the globe, through a combination of colonization, trade networks, the endeavors of Christian missionaries, and latterly, the media. Thus, the Christmas customs of the northern Europeans were exported to the farthest outposts of the planet, bringing curious images of reindeer, frosted windows, pine trees, and red-faced Santas to the tropics, the deserts, the atolls, and the savannahs. Driven by rampant commercialism, this Anglo-German-American version of Christmas has grown in scale and influence around the world, steamrolling and bulldozing many idiosyncratic local and regional customs to destruction, or pushing them to the fringes of their indigenous cultures. The celebration of Christmas has become globalized. Peculiarities and differences remain, but they are not as widespread or pronounced as they once were.

* * * *

CHRISTMAS DAY IN ANTARCTICA is celebrated in 24-hour daylight. In spite of its falling in midsummer, those living there (scientists in snowsuits mainly) can still guarantee a white Christmas—for the time being at least.

THE FIRST OFFICIAL Christmas celebrated in Australia came in 1788 at Sydney Cove, as the British set about establishing the first penal colony on the land claimed for the Crown by Captain Cook a few years earlier. There was, however, little to cheer anyone that year—except convict Michael Dennison. He had been sentenced to **200 lashes** for stealing a pound of flour but, in the festive spirit of peace and goodwill, he had his penalty reduced to just 150 lashes.

* * * *

A BOILED PIG'S HEAD, OR SNOUT, with mashed-up barley was a Christmas Eve specialty in Latvia for centuries. The dish, known as *kuki*, is not so popular these days.

IN AUSTRALIA, AS IN OTHER SOUTHERN HEMISPHERE COUNTRIES, THE Christmas holiday falls at the height of summer and it's not unusual for people to be carving up the turkey and opening their presents in temperatures touching three figures Fahrenheit. Many Christmas dinners and parties take the form of a **barbecue on the beach** or in the backyard, with the turkey cooked over the coals either whole or in marinated pieces or kebabs. In the absence of snow, many Australian children compromise by making "sandmen" on the beach.

❄ ❄ ❄ ❄

OVER 70 MAJOR **BUSH FIRES** RAGED ACROSS AUSTRALIA ON CHRISTMAS Day 2001, with 5,000 firefighters on duty, and 20,000 helpers preoccupied with containing and extinguishing the blazes. It took over three weeks for the fires to be brought under control.

❄ ❄ ❄ ❄

THE CELEBRATION OF CHRISTMAS IN THE LARGELY CATHOLIC countries of South and Central America is a more overtly religious, and less commercial, affair than it has become in other Western countries. Nativity scenes, street processions, and the attendance of church services (especially Midnight Mass) form the focus of the holiday period. In **Brazil** Christmas takes place in the summer and the main feast is eaten outdoors, often on the beach. Many Brazilian cooks marinate their turkey in rum, onions, garlic, tomatoes, lime juice, and other spices, and serve it with colored rice.

❄ ❄ ❄ ❄

IN RECENT TIMES THE CELEBRATION OF CHRISTMAS BY CHINA'S **roughly 50 million Christians** has become a more visible cultural event. Markets and shops have started stocking Western-style Christmas paraphernalia such as cards, trees, and traditional gifts as the commercialism of the festival seeps into China's wider community. Children hang up stockings for Dun Che Lao Ren or Lan Khoong (Father Christmas), who can also be found in various shopping malls across the country. Christianity is China's fastest-growing religion but it remains tightly controlled and closely watched by the authorities.

❄ ❄ ❄ ❄

CHRISTMAS WAS **OFFICIALLY ABOLISHED** IN CUBA BY THE COMMUNIST government in 1969, allegedly to avoid any disruption to the all-important sugar harvest. President Castro reinstated the holiday in 1997, but the celebrations have been rather muted as no one under the age of 40 or so has the faintest idea what to do with themselves. Since then, Cuba has experienced a minor religious revival, galvanized by the visit of Pope John Paul II, but Christmas Day still barely registers as an event of significance. Travel the streets of Havana on December 25, and Christmas decorations remain conspicuous by their absence.

WHILE MANY IN WESTERN EUROPE AND THE UNITED STATES PLUCK and hang their turkeys in preparation for the Christmas feast, the people of the Czech Republic, and others in Eastern Europe, get busy draining their ponds of carp. These **giant goldfish** traditionally form the centerpiece of the Czech Christmas meal and they are often kept in the bathtub until the last minute as they are tastiest when fresh, accompanied by a potato salad. Elsewhere in Central and Eastern Europe, especially in rural areas, the tradition of eating a 12-course meatless meal (one for each apostle) is still observed.

❄ ❄ ❄ ❄

IN ETHIOPIA, CHRISTIANS USE THE OLD JULIAN CALENDAR AND celebrate Christmas on January 7, flocking to the town of Lalibela, built by a king of that name in the twelfth century as Ethiopia's own Jerusalem. Pilgrims travel for days, even weeks, to celebrate the feast day they know as Ganna, which takes its name from a form of hockey believed to have been played by the shepherds as they awaited news of Jesus's birth. Ganna is still played today and forms a big part of the colorful Christmas festivities, which also involve a great deal of singing, dancing, and drumming as well as more solemn ceremonies that are conducted in ancient churches carved into hillsides of volcanic rock.

FOR MANY CENTURIES THE SAUNA, A HUGELY IMPORTANT FEATURE
of **Finnish culture**, has played a central part in the country's
traditional celebration of Christmas. Today Finns still observe the
custom of taking a sauna on Christmas Eve, after which many choose
to visit the graves of their loved ones before settling down to a lavish
dinner. The sauna is an almost sacred institution in Finland and
historians now believe that their ancestors were using them as long
as 2,000 years ago. There are over **two million saunas** installed
throughout the country, the majority of them in private homes.
With a population of just five million, the Finns can boast that, by
a considerable distance, they have the highest sauna per capita ratio
on the planet.

❄ ❄ ❄ ❄

*There is nothing that Finns have been so unanimous
about as their sauna. This unanimity has remained
unbroken for centuries and is sure to continue as long as
there are children born in their native land, as long as
the invitation still comes from the porch threshold in the
evening twilight: "The sauna is ready."*

MAILA TALVIO (1871–1951), Finnish writer

❄ ❄ ❄ ❄

*I can see myself as a little girl, bundled up to the tip of my nose in
furs and knitted shawls, tiny wooden shoes on my feet, a lantern
in my hand, setting out with my parents for the Midnight Mass
of Christmas Eve.... We started off, a number of us, together in
a stream of light. Our lanterns cast great shadows on the white
road, crisp with frost. As our little group advanced it saw others
on their way, people from the farm and from the mill, who
joined us, and once on the Place de l'Église we found ourselves
with all the parishioners in a body. No one spoke—the icy north
wind cut short our breath; but the voice of the chimes filled
the silence.... We entered, accompanied by a gust of wind that
swept into the porch at the same time we did; and the splendours
of the altar, studded with lights, green with pine and laurel
branches, dazzled us from the threshold.*

THERESE BENTZON, "Christmas in France"
published in *The Century Magazine*, describing a Christmas c. 1840

ON CHRISTMAS EVE 1951, HUNDREDS OF FRENCH SCHOOLCHILDREN were part of a large crowd to witness the arresting sight of **Father Christmas being executed** by irate clergymen outside Dijon Cathedral. Against a background of resounding cheers, an eight-foot-high, straw-filled effigy of the jolly man from the North Pole was hanged from the cathedral railings and then set on fire at the beard. Posters were nailed up around the execution site, declaring: "This is not a boast nor a publicity stunt, but a loud and strong protest against a lie which is incapable of awakening religious sentiment in children." Dismayed by the growing commercialization and "paganization" of Christmas, the priests in the diocese of Dijon decided to make public their disappointment with a display of medieval-style brutality. What better symbol of gluttony to bear the brunt of their pious fury than the fat guy in the red suit with all the presents? The pro-Santa lobby in the Dijon district, however, was out in force the following day, forming a rally of their own in the city center and erecting a number of *Père Noël* effigies in the streets, including a large one on the roof of the City Hall.

❄ ❄ ❄ ❄

IN THE RURAL EAST OF THE NETHERLANDS, YOU MAY STILL HEAR AN eerie sound wafting over the flat fields from the start of Advent through to Epiphany. Some locals there continue to observe the ancient custom of **"blowing the midwinter horn"** to celebrate the coming of Christ. The meter-long horns, carved from elder branches by expert craftsmen, are blown over wells so that the noise will carry for miles around and, the blower hopes, will be answered by another in the distance. The practice is another example of Christians absorbing and reworking pagan traditions to their convenience. In pre-Christian times, the sound of the horn was believed to scare off evil spirits.

❄ ❄ ❄ ❄

*Roses are reddish*
*Violets are bluish*
*If it weren't for Christmas*
*We'd all be Jewish.*

BENNY HILL, English comedian

BRINGING AN ENTIRE PINE TREE INTO THE HOME AND DECORATING it with candles, gifts, and baubles is just one of several Christmas customs that have their origins in Germany. It was from there, too, that the British imported hundreds of ingenious **wooden and mechanical toys** in the nineteenth century as the fashion for Christmas gifts, under the tree and in stockings, began to take hold. The popularity of Christmas trees increased after 1774 when Goethe included the following description in his novel *The Sorrows of Young Werther*:

*He began talking of the delight of the children and of that age when the sudden appearance of the Christmas tree, decorated with fruit and sweets, and lighted up with wax candles, caused such transports of joy. "You too shall have a gift, if you behave well," said Charlotte, hiding her embarrassment behind a sweet smile.*

❄ ❄ ❄ ❄

*… But better than the Leipziger Messe, better even than a summer market at Freiburg or at Heidelberg is a Christmas market in any one of the old German cities in the hill country, when the streets and the open places are covered with crisp clean snow, and the mountains are white with it and the moon shines on the ancient houses and the tinkle of sledge bells reaches when you escape from the din of the market…. The air is cold and still, and heavy with the scent of the Christmas-trees brought from the forest for the pleasure of the children. Day by day you see the rows of them growing thinner, and if you go to the market on Christmas Eve itself you will find only a few trees left out in the cold. The market is empty, the peasants are harnessing their horses or their oxen, the women are packing up their unsold goods. In every home in the city one of the trees that scented the open air a week ago is shining now with lights and little gilded nuts and apples, and is helping to make that Christmas smell, all compact of the pine forest, wax candles, cakes, and painted toys, you must associate so long as you live with Christmas in Germany.*

MRS. ALFRED SIDGWICK
*Home Life in Germany,* 1908

GREENLAND, THE WORLD'S LARGEST ISLAND, IS ONE OF THE SEVERAL regions within the Arctic Circle that claim to be the home of Santa Claus. Rivals say the claims of the Danish dependency are undermined by the fact that there is not a single tree, let alone a proper Christmas tree, to be found the length and breadth of a land measuring over half the size of the entire European Union. It is, they say, just lichen, moss, and grass—and how on earth do you get presents under that? Greenlanders, of whom there are roughly 50,000, most of them working in the fishing industry, can at least boast two of the world's more unusual Christmas dishes: *mattak* and *kiviak*. *Mattak* is a strip of whaleskin with some blubber inside. It is said to taste a little like coconut, but as it's virtually impossible to chew most people just swallow it. Christmas is the one night of the year when Greenland's men look after the women, and they serve out the *mattak* after coffee which they even stir for the females. *Kiviak* is the raw flesh of the auk, an Arctic bird. It is wrapped in seal skin and buried under heavy stones for several months until it reaches a stage of decomposition from which its taste can only go downhill.

❄ ❄ ❄ ❄

THERE ARE OVER 30 MILLION CHRISTIANS LIVING IN THE INDIAN subcontinent, most of them along the coasts of the south and west and in the hill regions of the northeast. The customs of each region differ slightly but in the tropical plains of the south, Christians use **mango and banana trees** as the centerpiece of decorations in the home.

❄ ❄ ❄ ❄

IN 1984, TEMPERATURES IN WASHINGTON WERE IN THE MID-SEVENTIES when President Reagan turned on the lights at the traditional National Christmas Tree ceremony outside the White House.

IT IS AN ANCIENT TRADITION OF IRAQ'S ASSYRIAN CHRISTIAN community to light bonfires of thornbush on Christmas Eve in front of their homes or in their courtyards. If the thorns burn down to ash, it is thought to be good luck for the family in the coming year. Until the 2003 Gulf War, there were 1 million Christians living **in Iraq**, but, according to the U.S. International Commission on Religious Freedom, as many as half of them are believed to have fled the country as the sectarian violence escalated. As Advent got under way in 2006, the head of Iraq's Christians, Patriarch Emmanuel Delly, appealed to worshippers to refrain from public celebrations at Christmas on security grounds. Many Christians in Iraq were suspected by insurgents of being agents of the Coalition forces.

❄ ❄ ❄ ❄

THE NATIVITY FORMS THE FOCUS of Christmas celebrations in Italy, just as it does in Central and South America and other strongly Catholic cultures. Great effort and creativity goes into the arrangements of manger scenes, but there is little other evidence, in public at least, of Christmas festivities. Tens of thousands of worshippers come to Rome from abroad over the Christmas period—many of them to hear the Pope's Christmas address in St. Peter's Square—but they are often surprised by the absence of the gaudy Christmas decorations in shops and streets common in other Western cities and towns. Visitors might also be forgiven for thinking they have flown to Edinburgh by mistake when they hear the unmistakable bleating of the **bagpipes wafting across the piazza**. For centuries, Italian shepherds used to come down from the mountains of Abruzzo and Calabria to Rome and other cities, wearing sheepskin tops and leather breeches, to play their pipes in markets and squares. One other Christmas custom peculiar to the Italians is the belief among children that it is not Father Christmas but a kindly old witch called La Befana who delivers the gifts in the middle of the night. The legend goes that La Befana was following the Three Wise Men to Bethlehem when she got lost and has been wandering the earth ever since.

❄ ❄ ❄ ❄

## DIARY ENTRY, 26 December 1770

*In the pm myself, Mr. Banks [the botanist Joseph], and all the Gentlemen came on board, and at 6am weigh'd and came to sail with a light breeze at South-West. The* Elgin *Indiaman saluted us with 3 cheers and 13 Guns, and soon after the Garrison with 14, both of which we return'd. Soon after this the Sea breeze set in at North by West, which obliged us to Anchor just without the Ships in the Road. The number of Sick on board at this time amounts to 40 or upwards, and the rest of the Ship's Company are in a weakly condition, having been every one sick except the Sailmaker, an old Man about 70 or 80 years of age; and what is still more extraordinary in this man is his being generally more or less drunk every day. But notwithstanding this general sickness, we lost but 7 men in the whole: the Surgeon, 3 Seamen, Mr. Green's Servant, and Tupia and his Servant, both of which fell a sacrifice to this unwholesome climate before they had reached the object of their wishes. Tupia's death, indeed, cannot be said to be owing wholly to the unwholesome air of Batavia [Jakarta]; the long want of a Vegetable Diet, which he had all his life before been used to, had brought upon him all the Disorders attending a Sea life. He was a shrewd, sensible, ingenious man, but proud and obstinate, which often made his situation on board both disagreeable to himself and those about him, and tended much to promote the diseases which put a Period to his Life.*

CAPTAIN COOK

❄ ❄ ❄ ❄

THE NORWEGIAN LANDSCAPE IS CARPETED IN BILLIONS of pine trees, but it wasn't until the early twentieth century that the locals began to follow the German custom of bringing them into the home at Christmas. The traditional feast is eaten on Christmas Eve, after which it is customary for Norwegian families to hold hands and dance around the tree in a ring before opening their presents. Stocking presents are delivered in the night by a dwarf variety of Father Christmas, a bearded troll or gnome called Julenisse.

CHRISTMAS IS BIG IN JAPAN IN SPITE OF THE FACT THAT ONLY 1 PERCENT of the country is Christian. The country has a long history of copying ideas from other cultures and in recent decades Christmas has become a significant event in the Japanese calendar, even though it is not yet an official holiday. Many Japanese don't have the first clue what Christmas is about but they are perfectly happy to decorate their homes, put up Christmas trees, exchange gifts, sing along to "Ludolph the Lednosed Leindeer," and sit down to a special meal on December 25. (Following the example of the occupying Americans after World War II, many Japanese cook hamburgers or fried chicken.) Tradesmen and big corporations seem to be behind the growing popularity of Christmas, flooding the market with festive goods, and bedecking buildings with Western-style lights and adornments. The experience in Japan illustrates how easily Christmas is absorbed into alien cultures, mainly because it falls at the end of the year when many celebrations are already held. In Japan, you see a lot of drunk people staggering around the streets throughout December. Christmas is *bonenkai* season (literally, "forget-the-year-party"), when the Japanese eat and drink themselves daft, and wipe the slate on the year that has just passed.

NORWAY HAS A NUMBER OF PECULIAR CHRISTMAS TRADITIONS. THE last Sunday before Christmas in Norway is known as Dirty Sunday because houses are given a thorough cleaning, and anything metal or glass is polished and buffed in preparation for the holiday period. In the western coastal city of Bergen, the children of the surrounding area contribute to the construction of the world's largest gingerbread city. Each year the Norwegian youth pushes back the boundaries of gingerbread creativity and construction to produce ever more original additions to their sprawling confectionary conurbation. In among the traditional gingerbread houses and gingerbread men, there are gingerbread boats, gingerbread schools, gingerbread factories, gingerbread dogs, and gingerbread cars.

*Did you know that Christmas Day is absolutely the best day to fly? No crowded airports and crowded planes. I always flew to Australia. That's what Christmas was for me—a plane journey to the next tournament.*

MONICA SELES, tennis player

✳ ✳ ✳ ✳

CAPTAIN JOHN SMITH

CAPTAIN JOHN SMITH, LEADER OF THE FIRST English colony in the United States at Jamestown, spent Christmas 1607 as a captive of the local Algonquian Indians. He later claimed that the chief's beautiful daughter, Pocahontas, saved his life by throwing herself across his body just as he was about to be executed. Otherwise, he seemed to have a very jolly time of it in captivity, writing in his diary:

*The extreme winds, rayne, frost and snow caused us to keep Christmas among the savages, where we were never more merry, nor fed on more plenty of good Oysters, Fish, Flesh, Wild Fowl, and good bread, nor never had better fires in England.*

✳ ✳ ✳ ✳

IN THE CENTER OF CARACAS, the capital city of **Venezuela**, it is customary for the streets to be blocked off early in the morning during the Christmas period to allow the youth of the city to roller-skate to and from early Mass.

✳ ✳ ✳ ✳

FOR CENTURIES THE JEWISH communities of Central and Eastern Europe dreaded the Christmas period. Years of being attacked in the streets by drunken Christians taught them to stay in their homes, especially after dark, until the holiday period had passed.

# All the Trimmings
## Christmas Odds and Ends

*Like all intelligent people, I greatly dislike Christmas. It revolts me to see a whole nation refrain from music for weeks together in order that every man may rifle his neighbour's pockets under cover of a ghastly general pretence of festivity. It really is an atrocious institution this Christmas. We must be gluttonous because it is Christmas. We must be drunken because it is Christmas. We must be insincerely generous; we must buy things that nobody wants, and give them to people we don't like; we must go to absurd entertainments that make even our little children satirical; we must writhe under venal officiousness from legions of freebooters, all because it is Christmas—that is, because the mass of population, including the all-powerful middle-class tradesman, depends on a week of licence and brigandage, waste and intemperance, to clear off its outstanding liabilities at the end of the year.*

GEORGE BERNARD SHAW
*Music in London*

❋ ❋ ❋ ❋

*If a man called Christmas Day a mere hypocritical excuse for drunkenness and gluttony, that would be false, but it would have a fact hidden in it somewhere. But when Bernard Shaw says that Christmas Day is only a conspiracy kept up by poulterers and wine merchants from strictly business motives, then he says something which is not so much false as startling and arrestingly foolish. He might as well say that the two sexes were invented by jewellers who wanted to sell wedding rings.*

G. K. CHESTERTON
*George Bernard Shaw*

*He [George Bernard Shaw] writes like a Pakistani who
has learned English when he was twelve years old in
order to become a chartered accountant.*

JOHN OSBORNE
letter to the *Guardian*

When will artists and printers design us some Christmas cards that will be honest
and appropriate to the time we live in? Never was the Day of Peace and Good
Will so full of meaning as this year; and never did the little cards, charming as they
were, seem so formal, so merely pretty, so devoid of imagination, so inadequate
to the festival. This is an age of strange and stirring beauty, of extraordinary
romance and adventure, of new joys and pains. And yet our Christmas artists have
nothing more to offer us than the old formalism of Yuletide convention. After a
considerable amount of searching in the bazaars we have found not one Christmas
card that showed even a glimmering of the true romance, which is to see the beauty
or wonder or peril that lies around us. Most of the cards hark back to the stage-
coach up to its hubs in snow, or the blue bird, with which Maeterlinck penalized us
(what has a blue bird got to do with Christmas?), or the open fireplace and jug of
mulled claret. Now these things are merry enough in their way, or they were once
upon a time; but we plead for an honest romanticism in Christmas cards that will
express something of the entrancing color and circumstance that surround us today.
Is not a commuter's train, stalled in a drift, far more lively to our hearts than the
mythical stage-coach?

Or an inter-urban trolley winging its way through the dusk like a casket of
golden light? Or even a country flivver, loaded down with parcels and holly and the
Yuletide keg of root beer? Root beer may be but meagre flaggonage compared to
mulled claret, but at any rate 'tis honest, 'tis actual, 'tis tangible and potable. And
where, among all the Christmas cards, is the airplane, that most marvelous and
heart-seizing of all our triumphs? Where is the stately apartment house, looming
like Gibraltar against a sunset sky? Must we, even at Christmas time, fool ourselves
with a picturesqueness that is gone, seeing nothing of what is round us?

CHRISTOPHER MORLEY, American writer and humorist (1890–1957)
*Mince Pie*, 1918

THE GIVING OUT OF PRESENTS TO MEMBERS of the royal household became an important Christmas ritual at Windsor Castle during Queen Victoria's reign. On Christmas Eve, all members were invited to join the Queen and Prince Albert in a ceremony around one of the castle's huge, lavishly decorated trees. Each of the presents piled at the foot of the tree carried nametags with personal messages written by the Queen herself. The gifts were usually small but exquisite, the women receiving jewelry such as lockets and chains, while the men were given accessories such as pearl studs or gold waistcoat buttons. Each member was also given an engraving of the Queen and her family, a practical book such as an almanac, and a box of sweets. After the ceremony, the royal family retired to one of their three sitting rooms to exchange their own gifts in private. Between 1840 and 1857 Victoria gave birth to nine children (who produced a total of 40 children of their own), so the opening of gifts was often a rowdy affair, un-Victorian even. The Windsor House trees were so beautifully decorated that courtiers described them as works of art in their own right. Victoria and Albert had small trees just for themselves placed on tables. In her diary entry for Christmas Day 1850, the young Queen describes her embarrassment at the wealth of presents she received from her husband: *We all assembled and my beloved Albert first took me to my tree and table, covered by such numberless gifts, really too much, too magnificent.* The gifts included an oil painting by John Calcott Horsley, the man who drew the first Christmas card a few years earlier, and a bracelet designed by Albert himself which included a miniature portrait of their daughter Princess Louise.

## The Christmas tree

⋆ Growing Christmas trees is big business. In the United States, there are more than 20,000 Christmas tree growers and over 12,000 cut-your-own farms. Trees are grown in all 50 states, including Hawaii. In the UK, over 7 million trees are grown every year.

⋆ Each year more and more Christmas trees are being recycled for the benefit of the environment. They are used to make soil erosion barriers and also placed in ponds and lakes for fish shelter.

⋆ Christmas trees take an average of seven to ten years to mature.

⋆ It's best not to burn your Christmas tree in the fireplace. The resinous "green" wood causes creosote to build up, increasing the risk of a chimney fire.

*CHRISTMAS CREEP—NOUN.* (1) THE COMMERCIAL PHENOMENON whereby retailers push Christmas earlier and earlier in the year in order to lengthen the selling season and steal a march on their rivals. (2) Slightly weird guy from accounting, who dresses up in hilarious Santa Claus uniform for the office party, makes a drunken pass at the marketing director, and, around midnight, collapses into the buffet table with his face in a bowl of mashed potatoes.

The American poet Henry Wadsworth Longfellow wrote the famous carol "I Heard the Bells on Christmas Day" on December 25, 1864, during the Civil War, after hearing the news that his son, Charles, had been wounded in battle. Englishman John Baptiste Calkin put the poem to music eight years later, leaving out the two verses specifically about the war.

CHRISTMAS STRESS IS MORE THAN just a hollow expression or an excuse for hard-pressed journalists to fill up the column inches, at least according to a raft of surveys and polls in recent years. The research suggests that most of us do get seriously wound up at Christmas—the very time of year that is supposed to bring us a bit of peace and happiness after a twelve-month slog to the end of the calendar. The British Heart Foundation says that 85 percent of people show significant symptoms of stress while Christmas shopping; 14 percent of us feel stressed by our neighbors' outdoor light displays, according to research by the Halifax bank. Perhaps most depressing and alarming of all, however, is the finding that the stress starts to hit shoppers at around midday on the first Saturday of December. Researchers at Greenwich University say that, by lunchtime on "Black Saturday," our festive goodwill has been suffocated by the stress of finding Granny a knitted hat. From then on, the experts claim, the stress mounts and it doesn't go away until the holidays are over. And a Happy New Year to you too.

❄ ❄ ❄ ❄

"CHRISTMAS SHOPPING TURNS FROM A PLEASURE INTO A CHORE THAT raises our heart rates, shuts down body functions like our digestive systems and leaves us physically and mentally exhausted," says stress expert Neil Shah of the Stress Management Society. "Research shows that people get particularly stressed when they feel powerless. Shopping is no different."

## Stress Management Society tips to beat Christmas stress

★ Do all your shopping on one day. Write a list of who you are buying for, then shop via the Internet as much as possible to avoid crowds, lines, and parking problems.

★ Don't stop for coffee. Caffeine prompts the body to release cortisol, the stress hormone, which will leave you feeling tense. Instead take a bottle of water with you to keep yourself hydrated.

★ Whenever you are in a line, try this exercise: breathe in for 4 counts, hold it for 16 counts, then breathe out for 8 counts. This will focus your mind away from your immediate situation and boost the levels of serotonin in your brain.

WHEN YOU FINALLY CHUCK THE TURKEY CARCASS ON THE floor for your grandma and the dog to fight over, get up and burp your way into the living room to watch *It's a Wonderful Life*, pause a moment to reflect on the damage you and your family have just inflicted on the environment. Of the 8 million Christmas trees we buy each year, three-quarters are burned or dumped in landfill. (A round of applause for the 2 million people who go to the small-to-medium effort of taking their trees to a recycling depot.) More than a billion Christmas cards and 83 square kilometers of wrapping paper, an area the size of Paris, will suffer the same fate; over 3,000 tons of aluminum foil for the turkey, the equivalent of 20 jumbo jets, will end up being buried in the ground, and almost 50 percent of the toys you give your children will be thrown out by Easter.

FOR DECADES PEOPLE HAVE BEEN SPENDING BEYOND THEIR BUDGETS at Christmas but in recent years debt levels in Britain have soared, causing significant problems for thousands of individuals and households. In January 2007, 1.2 million bills went unpaid as spending sprees and early December payments hit people's pockets in the New Year. Credit cards and council tax are the bills that the hard-up are most likely to skip paying, followed by cell phones and utilities. The Citizens Advice Bureau saw an increase of 15 percent in people coming to discuss debt problems compared to January 2006. A quarter of all those who walked into their office in the financial year 2005–2006 had got themselves into debt difficulties.

## Credit Crunch Christmas Tips

★ Avoid borrowing further to try to pay off existing debt.

★ Talk to your creditors. They will sometimes be more understanding than you expect.

★ Work out how much you owe and then prioritize your payments.

★ Only offer to pay off debts at a rate that suits you. Don't get panicked into offering more than you can afford.

★ Don't pay for debt advice. Citizens Advice, independent experts in dealing with creditors, will help you for free.

★ Set up a standing order to save a little each month, and slowly build up a fund for Christmas or holidays.

YORKSHIRE FOLK BEGIN THEIR CHRISTMAS SHOPPING LATER THAN anyone else in Britain. Over a third of people living in "God's Own County" wait until Christmas Eve before hitting the shops. Yorkshire people are also among the lowest Christmas spenders of the regions in the UK.

## Christmas tree tips

because they dry out quickly in centrally heated homes, or they are placed in rooms with open fires. Your tree will last longer if you stand it up in a bucket of stones and water it every few days or so.

★ It's hard to tell the age of a Christmas tree by looking at it, so shake it to see if the needles fall off, or run your fingers along a branch against the flow.

★ Weight is another telltale sign. Fresh trees are much heavier than older ones because they're still full of sap.

★ If you plant a root-balled or container tree after Christmas, bear in mind that most pine trees are vigorous growers that reach great heights.

★ Many trees look as if they were grown in Chernobyl by Christmas Day

★ When discarding your tree, avoid carpeting your house in millions of needles by wrapping it in a sheet before carrying it outside.

★ Bushy trees with lots of dense branches look better wrapped in tinsel, while the more sparsely branched varieties suit just a few wisps of tinsel and lots of hanging decorations. Don't ask why.

IT'S BEST TO PICK HOLLY A FEW WEEKS BEFORE YOU intend to use it as a decoration and then store it because if you leave it much later than early December the birds will have stolen all the berries. To keep it fresh, treat holly like cut flowers and place the stems in a vase of water, or stick them into a bucket of moist sand. Holly will stay fresher for longer if, as with your tree, you keep the stems away from dehydrating heat sources like radiators and out of direct sunlight.

*Gentlemen do not care for the pretty trifles and decorations that delight ladies; and as for real necessities, they are apt to go and buy anything that is a convenience just as soon as it is discovered. Knick-knacks, articles of china, etc., are generally useless to them. A Lady cannot give a gentleman a gift of great value because he would certainly feel bound to return one still more valuable and thus her gift would lose all its grace and retain only a selfish commercial aspect.*

*What, then, shall she give? Here is the woman's advantage. She has her hands, while men must transact all their present giving in hard cash. She can hem fine handkerchiefs—and in order to give them intrinsic value, if their relationship warrants such a favour, she can embroider the name or monogram with her own hair. If the hair is dark it has a very pretty, graceful effect, and the design may be shaded by mingling the different hair of the family. We knew a gentleman who for years lost every handkerchief he took to the office; at length his wife marked them with her own hair, and he never lost another. Such gifts are made precious by love, time and talent.*

*The bare fact of rarity can raise an object commercially valueless, to an aesthetic level. Souvenirs from famous places or of famous people, a bouquet of wild thyme from Mount Hymettus, an ancient Jewish shekel or Roman coin, etc. All such things are very suitable as presents to gentlemen and will be far more valued than pins, studs, etc., which only represent a certain number of dollars and cents. Do not give a person who is socially your equal a richer present than he is able to give you. He will be more mortified than pleased. But between equals it is often an elegance to disregard cost and depend on rarity, because gold cannot always purchase it. Still between very rich people presents should also be very rich or else their riches are set above their friendship and generosity.*

Harpers Bazaar, 1879

# Martha Stewart's
# Christmas holiday to-do list

**December 1:** *Blanch carcass from Thanksgiving turkey. Spray paint gold, turn upside down, and use as a sleigh to hold Christmas cards.*

**December 2:** *Contact local choir to record outgoing Christmas message for answering machine.*

**December 3:** *Repaint Sistine Chapel ceiling with mocha trim.*

**December 4:** *Get new eyeglasses. Grind lenses self.*

**December 5:** *Fax family Christmas newsletter to Pulitzer committee for consideration.*

**December 6:** *Debug Windows '95.*

**December 9:** *Align carpets to adjust for curvature of Earth.*

**December 11:** *Lay Fabergé egg.*

**December 12:** *Take dog apart. Disinfect. Reassemble.*

**December 13:** *Collect dentures. They make excellent pastry cutters, particularly for decorative piecrusts.*

**December 14:** *Install plumbing in gingerbread house.*

**December 15:** *Adjust legs of chairs so all Christmas dinner guests will be the same height when sitting down.*

**December 16:** *Dip sheep and cows in egg whites and roll in powdered sugar to add a festive sparkle to the pasture.*

**December 17:** *Drain city reservoir; refill with mulled cider, orange slices, and cinnamon sticks.*

**December 18:** *Float votive candles in toilet tank.*

**December 20:** *Seed clouds for white Christmas.*

**December 21:** *Do festive good deed. Go to several stores. Be seen engaged in last-minute Christmas shopping, thus making many people feel less inadequate than they really are.*

**December 23:** *Organize spice racks by genus and phylum.*

**December 24:** *Build snowman in exact likeness of God.*

**December 25:** *Bear son. Swaddle. Lay in color-coordinated manger scented with homemade potpourri.*

**New Year's Eve:** *Give staff their resolutions. Call a friend in each time zone of the world as the clock strikes midnight in that country.*

ANONYMOUS

179

IN 1975, AMERICAN SELF-IMPROVEMENT GURU AND LIFE COACH WERNER Erhard set a world record of handwriting 62,824 Christmas cards from his home in San Francisco. He was very disappointed to receive only three in return. (Just kidding, Werner, I'm sure you got loads.)

＊ ＊ ＊ ＊

*Once again, we come to the Holiday Season, a deeply religious time that each of us observes, in his own way, by going to the mall of his choice.*

ANONYMOUS

＊ ＊ ＊ ＊

*I stopped believing in Santa Claus when I was six. Mother took me to see him in a department store and he asked for my autograph.*

SHIRLEY TEMPLE (1928– ), American actress and diplomat

＊ ＊ ＊ ＊

*As Christmas decorations are "but for a season" it is not necessary that they should be of expensive materials, or elaborate workmanship; on the contrary, the cheapness and simplicity of the means used in producing the effect, seem often to enhance the pleasure received from looking upon it.*

*Cassell's Book of the Household,*
1878

＊ ＊ ＊ ＊

*I love Christmas. I receive a lot of wonderful presents I can't wait to exchange.*
HENRY YOUNGMAN (1906–1998)
British-American comedian

*For common gifts, necessity makes pertinences and beauty every day, and one is glad when an imperative leaves him no option, since if the man at the door have no shoes, you have not to consider whether you could procure him a paint-box. And as it is always pleasing to see a man eat bread, or drink water, in the house or out of doors, so it is always a great satisfaction to supply these first wants. Necessity does everything well.... Next to things of necessity, the rule for a gift, which one of my friends prescribed, is, that we might convey to some person that which properly belonged to his character, and was easily associated with him in thought. But our tokens of compliment and love are for the most part barbarous. Rings and other jewels are not gifts, but apologies for gifts. The only gift is a portion of thyself. Thou must bleed for me. Therefore the poet brings his poem; the shepherd, his lamb; the farmer, corn; the miner, a gem; the sailor, coral and shells; the painter, his picture; the girl, a handkerchief of her own sewing. This is right and pleasing, for it restores society in so far to its primary basis, when a man's biography is conveyed in his gift, and every man's wealth is an index of his merit. But it is a cold, lifeless business when you go to the shops to buy me something, which does not represent your life and talent, but a goldsmith's. This is fit for kings, and rich men who represent kings, and a false state of property, to make presents of gold and silver stuffs, as a kind of symbolical sin-offering, or payment of black-mail....*

*He is a good man who can receive a gift well. We are either glad or sorry at a gift, and both emotions are unbecoming. Some violence, I think, is done, some degradation borne, when I rejoice or grieve at a gift. I am sorry when my independence is invaded or when a gift comes from such as do not know my spirit, and so the act is not supported; and if the gift pleases me overmuch, then I should be ashamed that the donor should read my heart, and see that I love his commodity and not him. The gift, to be true, must be the flowing of the giver unto me, correspondent to my flowing unto him. When the waters are at level, then my goods pass to him, and his to me. All his are mine, all mine his. I say to him, How can you give me this pot of oil, or this flagon of wine, when all your oil and wine is mine, which belief of mine this gift seems to deny? Hence the fitness of beautiful, not useful things for gifts.*

RALPH WALDO EMERSON (1803–1882)
*Essays and English Traits,* 1844

❄ ❄ ❄ ❄

THE UNITED STATES HAS TWO VARIETIES OF NATIVE MISTLETOE: THE American mistletoe, the one we kiss under, and the dwarf mistletoe, which has grown in forests for at least 20,000 years. Most mistletoe species are found in the western United States, providing food, shelter, and nesting sites for all sorts of creatures, including three types of butterfly that are entirely dependent on the plant for their survival. Squirrels, chipmunks, and even porcupines are known to eat mistletoe.

An ornament in which children delight, the idea of which comes from Germany, is a jolly little black chimney sweep, with his funny broom held high in the air. He wears a peaked white hat and carries a bag filled with goodies. He is made entirely of prunes—one for the head, two for the body, one for each arm, one for each hand, two for each leg, and one for each foot. The prunes are strung together with a coarse needle and thread. If, when made, he is too limber, give him a backbone by running a slender stick through the back of his head and body. Give him a paper hat shaped like a wide-mouthed horn, and make a paper face; then tie the sheer white bag across his shoulders, fasten it at the side with a pin and fill the bag with sweets; the broom can be fashioned of a wooden toothpick with a bunch of broom straws bound on one end. The happy child who receives him from the tree may devour the prunes when tired of the toy.

*The Delineator Magazine.* December 1901

❄ ❄ ❄ ❄

What funny things to give a baby—gold and myrrh and frankincense. That's men all over! It wouldn't cross their minds to bring a shawl!

Moira Andrew, poet and author

❄ ❄ ❄ ❄

Christmas started going wrong for me when I was about 14. All I wanted was some clothes, some money, some make-up, some jewellery, some perfume, some platforms, some tights, some electric curlers, a handbag, a leather jacket, a Jackie annual, a selection box, a Pick of the Pops album featuring a girl on the cover wearing kinky boots full of really bad cover versions, a stereo, a telly for my room, and my own front door key. What I actually got was an anglepoise lamp so that I didn't strain my eyes whilst I did my homework. My mother ended up with that anglepoise lamp—she wore it all Christmas Day, tightly wrapped around her neck.

Jenny Eclair (1960– ), English comedian
*The Book of Bad Behaviour*

# Acknowledgments

The author and publishers are grateful for permission to reproduce extracts from the following:

*The Diaries of Bernard Shaw, Our Theatres in the Nineties,* and *Music in London* by Bernard Shaw, reprinted by permission of the Society of Authors, on behalf of the Bernard Shaw Estate.

*The Book of Bad Behaviour* by Jenny Eclair, copyright © 2004 by Jenny Eclair, Virgin Books Ltd.

*Cider with Rosie* by Laurie Lee, copyright © 1959 by Laurie Lee, reprinted by permission of PFD on behalf of the Estate of Laurie Lee.

Excerpt from *The Diaries of Evelyn Waugh* (copyright © by Evelyn Waugh) reproduced by permission of PFD on behalf of Evelyn Waugh.

*Mince Pie* by Christopher Morley reproduced with permission of the Christopher Morley Literary Estate.

*A Better Class of Person* and a letter to the *Guardian* by John Osborne, reprinted by permission of the Arvon Foundation.

# Index